The American Constitutional System ❦

**FOUNDATIONS OF AMERICAN GOVERNMENT
AND POLITICAL SCIENCE**

Joseph P. Harris, Consulting Editor

The purpose of this series is to provide a group of relatively short treatises on major aspects of government in modern society. Each volume introduces the reader to a major field of political science through a discussion of important issues, problems, processes, and forces and at the same time includes an account of American political institutions. Each is the work of a distinguished scholar who is a specialist in and teaches the subjects covered. Together the volumes can well serve the needs of introductory courses in American government and political science.

ANDREW HACKER: The Study of Politics: The Western Tradition and American Origins

C. HERMAN PRITCHETT: The American Constitutional System

HUGH A. BONE and AUSTIN RANNEY: Politics and Voters

ROWLAND EGGER and JOSEPH P. HARRIS: The President and Congress

JOHN J. CORSON and JOSEPH P. HARRIS: Public Administration in Modern Society

CHARLES O. LERCHE, JR.: America in World Affairs

CHARLES R. ADRIAN: Governing Our Fifty States and Their Communities

THE AMERICAN CONSTITUTIONAL SYSTEM

C. Herman Pritchett
The University of Chicago

McGRAW-HILL BOOK COMPANY, INC.
NEW YORK / SAN FRANCISCO /
TORONTO / LONDON

**THE AMERICAN
CONSTITUTIONAL SYSTEM**

*This book is set in linotype Janson. The
original specimen sheets date from about
1700 and are of Dutch origin. The chapter
openings are Century Bold Condensed and
the displayed heads are News Gothic Bold.*

Preface

This book deals with the document which is the legal basis for all power exercised by the national government of the United States. The purpose of this volume is to describe in broad outlines the structure, functions, powers, and limitations of the American governmental system—the fundamental understandings about American governmental structure and power.

In all countries the basic framework of public authority is referred to as that country's constitution. The Constitution of the United States is a written document drafted in 1787, which became operative in 1789. It provides for the institutions of the Presidency, the Congress, and the Federal courts. It regulates the relationships between the national government and the states, and prescribes in more or less general terms their respective spheres of authority. It enumerates legal protections for rights of person and property.

Other studies in this series deal in more detail with the operation and interrelation of American governmental institutions. This volume has a broader purpose: to spell out the authoritative foundations for the operative governmental system, and to show how the provisions of the Constitution have been effective in shaping the development of our national institutions.

The drafters of the Constitution faced the challenge of planning a new nation with courage and vision. Their wisdom has been proved by time, which has made of the document they framed the oldest written constitution now in effect. However, the credit for this achievement rests not only with the founders, but also with those who have operated the American governmental system and given life to the constitutional provisions over the long period since 1789. This short book cannot undertake to *present even a summary of that constitutional history. But it may convey some conception of the Constitution as the instrument and symbol of American democratic government.*

C. Herman Pritchett

Contents

THE AMERICAN CONSTITUTION

Chapter 1

The Constitution of the United States of America was drafted between May 14 and September 17, 1787, by 55 men meeting in the city of Philadelphia. It was made effective on June 21, 1788, by the vote of nine state ratifying conventions. Under the governmental system set up by this document, a group of thirteen sparsely populated states strung out along the Atlantic Ocean from Massachusetts to Georgia has developed into one of the great powers of world history. Appropriately, the parchment sheets on which the Constitution was written are preserved as a national shrine in the National Archives at Washington, and the document has come to be regarded with the awe and reverence usually reserved for religious objects.

The Constitution has great value as a symbol of unity for a nation of vast expanse and diverse interests. But as an instrument of government its language has had to be given life and meaning by the events that have occurred since 1789. Congress animates the Constitution every time it passes a law or holds a hearing. The President construes the Constitution whenever he makes a decision, issues an executive order, or signs a bill into law. The Constitution of the United States is the body of practice built up during the past decades by the executive departments. It is manifested in the historic crises that have been met—Lincoln facing the disintegration of the Union, Roosevelt facing the collapse of the national economy. It is discoverable equally at lower levels, in the routines and the customs of public life, in what Justice Holmes called the inarticulate premises of a nation and a people.

The men who wrote the Constitution were seeking to create a government strong enough for protection against foreign enemies, preservation of the peace internally, and fostering of commercial development and the general welfare. At the same time, they did not want a national government which would be so strong as to obliterate the states or threaten individual rights of liberty and property. They were seeking to establish a system of *constitutional* government.

WHAT IS CONSTITUTIONAL GOVERNMENT?

Until the eighteenth century, the term "constitution" usually meant the general system of laws, institutions, and customs pertaining to the government of a country. The French and American Revolutions, however, brought a new concept of constitution into existence. The constitutional system was no longer to be the product of evolutionary processes. It was not to be deduced from a nation's history or practice. Rather, a constitution was a formal, written instrument, a "social contract" drafted by a representative assembly and ratified by a special procedure for determining public assent. A constitution was the act of a people constituting a government. The constitution brought the government into existence and was its source of authority. The government was the creature of the constitution.

To one accustomed to the older developmental view of constitutions, this was a disturbing departure. The Englishman Arthur Young, writing in 1792, spoke with contempt of the French and American idea of a constitution—"a new term they have adopted; and which they use as if a constitution was a pudding to be made by a recipe." To an Englishman it was obvious that a constitution could not be made; it had to grow.

Actually, of course, constitutions can combine both qualities. The Constitution of the United States was made in the summer of 1787, but it incorporated a tremendous amount of political experience from the past, and has been growing ever since. English experience has demonstrated that a democratic political system can develop and individual liberties be protected as well with a traditional unwritten constitution as with the newfangled recipe type of constitution. We have even come to see that there may be actually little difference between written and unwritten constitutions—the written one is constantly being reinterpreted and revised by practice and unwritten custom, while the principles of the unwritten constitution are constantly being reduced to writing in statutes, judicial decisions, and constitutional commentaries.

Whether written or unwritten, a constitution has four main purposes. First, it must provide the structure of the governmental system, the organs and institutions of public authority. Second, it must authorize the powers which the government is to possess, and allocate them among the various branches and organs. Third, it must state the limitations on governmental power, for the essence of constitutionalism is the maintenance of a balance between authority and liberty, between governmental power and individual rights. Fourth, it must provide for some means other than violent revolution by which the constitutional design can be adapted to future necessities.

THE ARTICLES OF CONFEDERATION

The Constitution drafted in 1787 was actually the second American constitution. The first was the Articles of Confederation, drawn up in 1777 and adopted in 1781. Before that the colonies had cooperated in their struggle for independence through the Continental Congress, which performed the functions of a *de facto* government from 1775 to 1781—raising, directing, and financing armies, sending and receiving diplomatic agents, entering into treaties with foreign countries. Whether it had any legal power to perform these actions is another question. The people of the states did not conceive that they had surrendered any of their rights to the Congress, and no state government felt bound by its decisions. Delegates to the Congress, once the states were established, were appointed by the state legislatures and subject to their instructions.

It was generally agreed that a more effective intercolonial organization was required. A committee was appointed on June 12, 1776, to draw up a plan for a permanent confèderation. The Articles of Confederation were adopted and sent to the states in November, 1777. Ratification by every state was required to make them binding, and Maryland, the thirteenth state, did not sign until March 1, 1781, at which time the Articles came into effect.

The framework of government set up by the Articles was quite simple. Virtually all functions were concentrated in a single legislative chamber, called a Congress. There was no second branch of the legislature and no separation of executive from legislative powers. Congress was to appoint such committees and civil officers as might be needed to carry on executive work, and it could provide courts for the limited purposes of dealing with disputes between states and captures and felonies on the high seas.

The authority of the Congress did not rest with the people, but with the state legislatures which had created it. Each state legislature chose and paid its delegates to the Congress, and each state had one vote. A two-thirds vote of the state delegations was required for the adoption of important measures, and amendments to the Articles required the unanimous consent of the states.

The Articles did specify certain rules of interstate comity to which the states were pledged. But the essential powers necessary to an effective central government were denied to the Confederation. The Congress could not levy taxes; it could only make a "requisition" on each state for its share of the estimated monetary needs of the union. The Congress could not regulate interstate commerce; and although it could make commercial treaties with foreign nations, the states felt free to retaliate against countries which discriminated against their trade. Finally, the Congress could not act directly on the citizens; it had to depend on the state governments for the execution of its measures. The Confederation could scarcely be called a government. As the Articles truthfully stated, it was a league of friendship entered into by sovereign states.

Such a weak government proved quite inadequate to the problems it faced. With no power of taxation, the public finances were soon in a hopeless state. With no power to regulate internal trade, the states taxed each other's goods in discriminatory fashion. Since the Confederation had no powers for dealing with the Revolutionary economic inflation, full pressure of the debtor class fell on the states, and in seven state legislatures programs authorizing the payment of debts with paper money were adopted. When such a plan was defeated in Massachusetts, farmers under the leadership of Daniel Shays resorted to violence, breaking up court sessions trying debt cases and attempting to seize arms from the government arsenal in Springfield.

Shays' Rebellion was most effective in convincing the conservative and the propertied that there were serious defects in the government both of the states and the Confederation. The revolutionary enthusiasm for the legislature as the dominant branch of government had diminished. Now responsible citizens were looking for some way of checking the legislatures. The post of state governor was still too weak for this purpose, and a system of judicial review of legislation had not yet been developed. The only effective control over state radicalism appeared to be a strengthening of the central government. In 1785 a meeting of representatives from Virginia and Maryland was held at Washington's home at Mount Vernon, for the purpose of discussing joint problems of navigation on Chesapeake Bay and the Potomac. Ignoring a provision in the Articles which required congressional consent to all agreements between states, they developed a plan for uniformity of import duties, commercial regulations, and currency in the two states.

When the Maryland legislature accepted these proposals in December, 1785, it suggested that Pennsylvania and Delaware be invited to join in the plan. In Virginia, Madison saw the possibility of using this initiative to get a general meeting on commercial problems, which the Virginia assembly proposed should meet at Annapolis in September, 1786. Nine states appointed delegates to go to Annapolis, but only five were present at the opening session. They waited three weeks for more delegates and then adjourned. But a report was drafted and sent to every state legislature and to Congress, suggesting that the states designate commissioners to meet in Philadelphia in May, 1787, "to take into consideration the situation of the United States, to devise such further provisions as shall appear to them necessary to render the Constitution of the Federal Government adequate to the exigencies of the Union."

Congress at first ignored the project, but in February, 1787, recommended a convention at the time and place already set, to meet for the "sole and express purpose of revising the Articles of Confederation," and of reporting to the Congress such alterations as would "render the federal constitution adequate to the exigencies of government, and the preservation of the union." Thus the official status of the Philadelphia Convention was merely that of a body advisory to Congress.

THE CONSTITUTIONAL CONVENTION

The Constitutional Convention met on May 28, 1787, and continued its deliberations until the completed document was ready for signature on September 17. Some 74 delegates were appointed, but only 55 ever attended the sessions. Every state except Rhode Island was eventually represented. With George Washington as the presiding officer, the delegates were a notable assemblage. They were comparatively young men, only twelve being over fifty-four years of age, and six were under thirty-one. Almost half were college graduates. They were almost without exception men of substance and position in the new country—lawyers, physicians, planters, merchants. Most of them had risked their necks in prominent military or civilian posts during the Revolution. But the fact that only eight of the fifty-six signers of the Declaration of Independence were in the Constitutional Convention is evidence that making a constitution enlisted different talents and interests from those required for making a revolution.

In the Convention, votes were cast by states. The proceedings were secret, and knowledge of what occurred is very largely due to the extensive notes which James Madison kept. Almost immediately after assembling, a complete and far-reaching plan for establishing a new national government was presented by the Virginia delegation. The Virginia Plan called for a bicameral legislature, with representation in both houses on the basis of population. The congress was to have sweeping legislative powers of its own as well as the power to veto all state laws which it regarded as going beyond state authority. The congress was to select the national executive, and a national judiciary was also contemplated. The executive and judiciary combined could constitute a "council of revision" with power to veto acts of the congress.

Delegates who found these proposals too sweeping countered with the so-called New Jersey Plan which was more on the pattern of the Articles of Confederation. There would continue to be a unicameral legislature in which each state would have equal representation, but the authority of the central government would be substantially increased by the addition of power to tax and to regulate commerce. Another important advance in this plan was that Federal laws and treaties were to be binding on the states. A Federal executive and judiciary were also provided.

The Convention after assembling turned itself into a committee of the whole and for three weeks mulled over these two plans. The New Jersey proposal was defeated on June 19. The members then reverted from committee status and, as a convention, began to go over again the various features of the Virginia Plan. One month of discussion produced agreement on a substantial number of points, so that on July 23 the Convention voted to set up a committee of detail which would draft a constitution embodying the principles agreed upon. This group, however, did more than redraft the Convention's resolutions into documentary form. It expanded some of the resolutions, and developed some entirely new provisions. The resulting document was presented to the Convention on August 6 and was the subject of further extended discussion. On September 17 the Constitution was signed by 39 of the 42 delegates present.

AMERICAN POLITICAL IDEAS

The ideas which went into the Constitution of the United States were drawn from the whole European political heritage of the new nation. The ideas themselves were not especially new nor were they creative inventions of the assembly. The genius of the Convention was rather in its practicality and willingness to compromise dogmatic principles rather than in any theoretical brilliance.

The Declaration of Independence has been generally regarded as the cornerstone of the American system of ideas about government, and the preeminent statement of American political theory. The basic conceptions had come from the English philosopher, John Locke, but the doctrines were sharpened and intensified by the experience of resistance to British rule. These principles were so much a part of American thinking that the Declaration referred to them as "self-evident." In addition to the Declaration, the constitutions of the new American states which were adopted between 1776 and 1780 abound in statements of the current political theory.

The first principle of the political thought of the time was that men are by nature endowed with certain inalienable rights. This conception assumed that a state of nature exists before the establishment of civil government. In this primeval condition all men are free, in the sense that they are subject to no one, and equal in the right to rule themselves.

A body of natural rights belongs to them as men, including the right to "life, liberty, and the pursuit of happiness." These rights not only antedate the existence of government; they are superior to it in authority. The exercise of coercive power by governments over men born free and equal can be justified only by the consent of the governed. The process as expressed by the Massachusetts Bill of Rights was that "the body politic is formed by a voluntary association of individuals: it is a social compact by which the whole people covenants with each citizen, and each citizen with the whole people, that all shall be governed by certain laws for the common good." The exact nature of the contract on which government was based, or the circumstances under which it was entered into, were little discussed, but this concept was given a sense of reality by the numerous written compacts which had figured in American development, especially the Mayflower Compact of 1620 and the colonial charters. The slogan, "no taxation without representation," was a particular application of the consent theory, with roots deep in English constitutional history.

Government is created by contract to serve the welfare of the people. To quote again the Massachusetts document, the aim of government is "to secure the existence of the body politic, to protect it, and to furnish the individuals who compose it with the power of enjoying in safety and tranquillity their natural rights, and the blessings of life." A government which fails to serve the ends for which it was set up has breached the contract under which it was established and forfeited the loyalty of its citizens. Thus the right of revolution, obviously fundamental to legitimizing the American action, was established. The Declaration of Independence stated the case as follows: "Whenever any form of government becomes destructive of these ends, it is the right of the people to alter or to abolish it, and to institute new government, laying its foundation on such principles and organizing its powers in such forms, as to them shall seem most likely to effect their safety and happiness."

The consequences of these basic political ideas quickly became visible in the constitutions adopted by the new states after 1776. Governmental power was limited in several ways. The royal governors had been the symbol of tyranny, so that the executive office in the new constitutions was deliberately weakened, while the legislature, symbol of resistance to foreign rule, was strengthened. In eight states the governor was chosen by the legislature, he had only a one-year term in ten states, his appointing power was generally limited, and he had the veto power in only three states. The one-year rule was common for all officials, not only for governors; as John Adams said, "where annual elections end, there tyranny begins."

The democratic theory professed in the new constitutions was not consistently practiced, however. Under the colonial government the lower classes had been rather generally excluded from political life. The revolutionary movement for a time gave promise of bringing the back-country folk and the unfranchised workers into the stream of politics, but actually the circle of power holders was little changed in the new state governments. Property and religious qualifications for office holding were general. Indeed, property, religious, and racial limitations were seemingly not regarded as inconsistent with the rights of man or the principles of political philosophy so eloquently stated in the Declaration of Independence.

CONSTITUTIONAL PRINCIPLES

These ideas were the foundation for the constitutional principles embodied in the instrument signed on September 17, 1787. First of all, the Constitution established a *republican* form of government. The monarchical principle had of course been completely discredited by colonial experience with George III, and republicanism was the revolutionary doctrine of the era. But there was considerable question in the minds of the founders as to how far the republican or representative principle should be carried. Direct election provided for the House of Representatives, but the Senate was to be chosen by the state legislatures. Likewise only a few of the delegates favored direct election of the President. Election by Congress was strongly supported, but eventually the Convention agreed on selection by electors chosen in each state as the legislature of that state might direct.

The only place where the term "republican" appears in the Constitution is in Article IV, which provides that the United States shall guarantee "a republican form of government" to every state in the Union, but the term is not there defined. Some have argued that since the United States was created as a republic, it is a serious mistake to think of our government as a "democracy." This position is usually taken by conservatives who treasure the aristocratic manifestations in the initial constitutional provisions, and who disapprove of modern trends toward egalitarianism, direct democracy, and mass society in general. Unquestionably an evolution has gone on which may be described as a change from a republic to a representative democracy, but this is a development which has occurred within the framework of constitutional principles.

Second, the Constitution set up a *federal* system. The delegates were in general agreement that a stronger central government had to be formed. Although their instructions were simply to revise the Articles of Confederation, it was obvious that the goals they had in mind required more fundamental changes.

Under the Articles, the central establishment was a confederation, a mere league of states, each of which retained its sovereign powers. The Constitution set up a new central government, which got its authority directly from the people, and was to exercise its powers directly on the people. The states retained their status and such of their powers as were not transferred to the national government. Naturally a central consideration at the Convention was to decide what powers would be so transferred, and how the division of functions would be described and enforced. The operation of a two-level governmental system has presented endless constitutional issues, the more important of which are discussed in Chapter 2, and one aspect of the relationship between the central government and the states had to be settled by a bloody civil war.

The federal principle was also at issue in the organization of the Congress. The large states, such as Virginia, Massachusetts, and Pennsylvania, were confident of their position in the new government and so supported the centralizing provisions of the Virginia Plan. The small states naturally feared the dominance of their larger neighbors, and wanted protection for their interests.

It was generally accepted that the House of Representatives would be elected by the people, and that membership would be proportionate to population. The Senate was to be elected by the state legislatures, and the large states wanted representation by population here also. But in the Congress under the Confederation, and in the Convention itself, each state had one vote, and the small states would not agree to a plan which did not preserve their status in some way. Finally on July 16 the Convention adopted the principle of equal state representation in the Senate by a vote of 5 to 4.

Third, the Constitution adopted the *separation of powers* principle. The first sentence of Article I vested "all legislative powers" in Congress, and the first sentences of Articles II and III similarly vested executive and judicial power in the President and in the courts, respectively. Each branch had its particular task—making the law, administering the law, enforcing the law. This division was in accord with the goal of limited government and was intended to make abuse of official power less likely.

For additional insurance, and with an eye to the realities of governmental operation, the founders infringed on strict separation of powers theory by a system of checks and balances which enabled each branch to have some say in the operation of the other two. The President could veto laws and appoint Federal justices. The Senate could confirm executive and judicial appointments and ratify treaties. Congress could control the kinds of cases to be heard by the Supreme Court. The courts could interpret congressional statutes and pass on the validity of executive acts.

Finally, basic to all the other ideas was that of *constitutionalism* itself, the conception that government power must be both authorized and limited by undertakings arrived at in advance, consented to by those affected, and given continuing validity by appropriate enforcement processes. The rule of law and of representative institutions with defined authority was to stand as a guarantee of individual liberty against the exercise of arbitrary governmental power.

RATIFICATION

The drafters of the Constitution realized that ratification of the document would present grave difficulties. The Articles of Confederation provided that revisions could be made only by a favorable vote of Congress and the approval of the legislatures in all 13 states. Rhode Island had not even sent delegates to the Convention, and there were other states where approval of the new Constitution was doubtful. Public opinion at the time was badly divided on the need for a stronger central government. In general the rural areas, the farmers and backwoodsmen, were quite suspicious, as a Massachusetts farmer put it, of "these lawyers, and men of learning, and moneyed men, that talk so finely, and gloss over matters so smoothly, to make us poor illiterate people swallow down the pill."

The drafters faced this problem boldly and developed in Article VII an entirely extralegal solution. They provided first that the Constitution should become effective on ratification by nine states. Second, ratification was to be by conventions in the states elected for this specific purpose. Third, the Constitution was not be presented to the Congress before being submitted to the states.

The use of state conventions for ratification purposes could be justified as providing a more democratic foundation for the new government, but it was also a practical means of bypassing hostile state legislatures unlikely to give up their own powers. The pro-Constitution forces sought to get the conventions elected as promptly as possible, before the opposition had a chance to organize. About three-fourths of the male white citizens over twenty-one failed to vote in the elections for convention delegates, Charles A. Beard estimates, either on account of their indifference or their disfranchisement by property qualifications.

One of the legacies of the ratification campaign was the most famous commentary on American government, *The Federalist*. These essays were newspaper articles written to influence the vote in the doubtful state of New York by Madison, Hamilton, and John Jay. Their discussions of the proposed Constitution have been generally thought to have had great influence at the time and have been widely accepted as authoritative guides to constitutional interpretation.

The Constitution was ratified by a wide majority in seven of the state conventions, but in the important states of Massachusetts, Virginia, and New York the voting was close. North Carolina and Rhode Island were the last two states to ratify. If a unanimous vote had been required to make the Constitution effective, it is probable that they would have stayed out, thus frustrating the entire effort.

The absence of a bill of rights was the most widespread criticism in the ratifying conventions, and in several doubtful states the promise that a bill of rights would be added was instrumental in securing the votes needed for ratification.

AMENDING THE CONSTITUTION

Since the Constitution was ratified, tremendous changes have occurred in the United States and in the world. Technical discoveries and inventions have affected the life of the country. Population has multiplied manyfold. The political party has undergone a transformation from a despised source of faction to an indispensable instrument of representative government. Public agencies have taken over responsibilities undreamed of in the eighteenth century. Standards of public morality have changed. How is a government of continental proportions and worldwide responsibilities, with a peacetime budget of over 90 billion dollars, to be accommodated within the confines of a document drafted 1¾ centuries earlier for the sparse population of 13 isolated states along the Atlantic seaboard?

One answer is that the framers of the Constitution were wise enough, and good enough politicians, to avoid the evil of too great specificity in drafting key provisions of the document. Their general intent was to stick to the fundamentals and to leave the implementation to subsequent legislative decision. In places they remained deliberately vague and thus avoided crystallization of opposition forces that would have been able to mobilize against concrete proposals. Thus no departmental setup for the executive branch was written into the Constitution. The question of a system of lower courts was left to Congress, as was the matter of presidential succession beyond the Vice President, and the time, place, and manner of electing representatives and senators. The powers given to the President and to Congress were typically stated in broad language.

Nevertheless, no amount of drafting skill could be expected to eliminate the necessity of revision and development to adapt the Constitution to the unforeseen and the unforeseeable. This adaptation has taken two forms—constitutional amendment and constitutional interpretation.

The presence of the amending clause was one of the factors which led Jefferson, originally inclined to oppose the Constitution, to decide in its favor. Since 1789 the procedures of Article V have been utilized to add 23 amendments to the Constitution. The first 10 of these amendments were drafted to meet the widespread protests against the absence of a bill of rights in the original Constitution, and were adopted in 1791.

Only 11 amendments have been added in the century since the Civil War. The Thirteenth, Fourteenth, and Fifteenth Amendments were adopted shortly after that conflict to abolish slavery and protect the rights of the newly freed Negroes. The Sixteenth and Seventeenth Amendments, both adopted in 1913, reflected the progressive political philosophy of the early twentieth century by authorizing the Federal income tax and providing for direct popular election of senators. The Eighteenth Amendment (1919), authorizing national prohibition, was repealed by the Twenty-first (1933). The Twenty-second Amendment (1951) limited the President to two terms in office, and the Twenty-third (1961) gave residents of the District of Columbia the right to vote in presidential elections.

Of the two methods which Article V provides for proposing amendments—by a two-thirds majority of each house of Congress, or by a convention summoned by Congress at the request of the legislatures of two-thirds of the states—only the former has been employed. Since a constitutional convention has never been called under Article V, there is no agreement as to the many questions that would arise concerning operation of such a convention.

If petitions were actually received from two-thirds of the state legislatures, there would be no means of forcing Congress to call the requested amending convention, and it can be anticipated that Congress would not welcome such an infringement on what has become one of its own prerogatives. If Congress did acquiesce, it would have to provide by statute for calling the convention. Whether legislation could in any way limit the powers of the convention is questionable, however. After assembling, the delegates might undertake to consider amendments to any part of the Constitution, or even propose an entirely new document, as the Convention of 1787 did. In view of all the uncertainties surrounding the convention provision, it is unlikely that this Pandora's box in Article V will ever be opened.

The ratification of all the amendments to the Constitution except one has been by vote of three-fourths of the state legislatures. Only in the case of the Twenty-first Amendment, which repealed the Eighteenth, did Congress require the use of state conventions. The reason for this exception was the fear in Congress that the overrepresentation in the state legislatures of rural areas, which tended to be "dry," might imperil adoption of the amendment, whereas conventions would more equitably represent the views of the urban areas.

Perhaps the most striking fact about the amending process is the infrequency with which it has been used. Excluding the initial ten amendments, which must be considered practically part of the original Constitution, amendments have been adopted at a rate of less than one per decade. Following the Civil War amendments, there was a period of over 40 years during which the Constitution appeared unamendable. This was an era of agrarian discontent, industrial unrest, and growing interest in political and economic reforms. The conservatism of the Supreme Court, symbolized by its invalidation of the income tax in 1895, made constitutional amendment seem a necessary step toward achieving liberal legislative goals.

In 1913, however, the long liberal campaign for the income tax and direct election of senators succeeded, and the women's suffrage amendment followed shortly thereafter. Also, adoption of the Eighteenth Amendment revealed the possibility of a small but dedicated pressure group exploiting the amending machinery successfully. With six amendments added to the Constitution between 1913 and 1933, the amending process no longer seemed so formidable. Moreover, the liberalization of the Supreme Court's views by President Franklin D. Roosevelt's appointments substantially eliminated liberal interest in further amendments.

After the 1930s pressure for amendments to the Constitution came almost entirely from conservative and reactionary political quarters. Interest of conservatives in the amending process was motivated by their loss of influence in all three branches of the government. The increase in executive power and congressional expenditures, the acceptance of new welfare functions internally and new responsibilities internationally by the Federal government, and the reduced role of the states were all trends which stimulated the resistance of various conservative groups. Lacking the power to block these developments through the normal political processes, they fell back on the device of constitutional amendment. During the 1950s the Bricker Amendment to limit the Federal government's power to enter into international agreements, as well as a proposal to place a ceiling on Federal income taxation, were conservative measures which failed of adoption.

The only amendment actually secured by this drive was the Twenty-second, adopted in 1951. This limitation of the President to two terms was initially proposed as a Republican measure after their party had suffered four defeats at the hands of President Roosevelt, but was subsequently supported by conservatives of both parties who feared strong executive leadership. Ironically, the first President to feel the effects of the amendment was a Republican, President Eisenhower.

INTERPRETING THE CONSTITUTION

More important than the amending process in adapting the Constitution to changing conditions is the device of constitutional interpretation. In fact, the possibility of gradual modification of constitutional meanings to meet new times and new necessities is the principal reason why resort to formal amendment has been relatively infrequent.

The process of constitutional adaptation is one which goes on at many levels and in many contexts. There are adaptations which develop on an entirely unplanned basis in the form of usage or customs or methods of procedure or institutions. Perhaps the most striking example in American history is the prompt development after 1789 of a party system, for which the framers had not planned, and which in fact they had taken some pains to try to prevent. The party system, with its tickets for President and Vice President, immediately required the remedial provisions of the Twelfth Amendment, but in no other respect has the written Constitution been changed to recognize the realities of party government. The development of committees in Congress, the rise of the Cabinet, the use of executive agreements instead of treaties, the assumption that representatives must be residents of the districts they represent in Congress—these and many other customs and usages were evolutionary adjustments of the constitutional system to practical problems with which it was confronted.

A much more intentional and sophisticated type of constitutional interpretation goes on in the decision making of the executive and legislative branches. When President Kennedy recommended Federal financial aid to the schools in 1961, he announced his view that public aid to religious schools was unconstitutional, and the Secretary of Health, Education and Welfare presented to Congress a legal brief indicating the administration's view as to what the constitutional problems were in Federal aid to education.

The most highly rationalized type of constitutional interpretation is that engaged in by judges, and particularly by the Supreme Court of the United States. Circumstances have given the Supreme Court recognition as the "official" interpreter of the Constitution, and its rulings are accepted as the best evidence of constitutional meanings. Although the Supreme Court and its members have often been attacked for individual decisions, judicial interpretation of the Constitution has been generally regarded as an essential safeguard of the constitutional system.

SUMMARY

The Constitution of the United States was drafted to provide a national government which would be strong enough to protect and develop those interests of defense, commercial welfare, and domestic security which the states were separately unable to achieve. The men who made it were generally of the opinion that government is a "necessary evil"; they were jealous of their individual rights and they had strong loyalties to their states. But experience had convinced them that if they did not all hang together they would all hang separately, and so the case for a central "government of powers" was clear to the leaders of opinion.

With all the conflicting interests that were involved, however, the Constitution had to be a product of compromises. Whereas individual liberties were of great concern to the drafters, their language was not explicit enough to satisfy the country, and a detailed bill of rights had to be added as a necessary condition to ratification. The fact that the framers created a government strong enough for national protection and advancement, at the same time preserving a significant role for the states and safeguarding the rights of individuals, is eloquent testimony to their success.

Review Questions

1. What novel problems did written constitutions create?

2. What are the main functions of a constitution?

3. What were the essential features of governmental organization under the Articles of Confederation?

4. Why was the Constitutional Convention called?

5. Contrast the two principal plans presented to the convention.

6. What were the basic political ideas of the Constitution?

7. Why was the Constitution not submitted to the state legislatures for ratification?

8. Why has the Constitution been amended so seldom?

9. Suggest some of the problems which might be faced if Congress ever summoned a convention to propose amendments to the Constitution.

10. How has the Constitution been kept up to date?

THE FEDERAL SYSTEM

Chapter 2

In essence, American federalism is a form of political organization in which the exercise of power is divided between two levels of government, each having the use of those powers as a matter of right, and each acting on the same citizen body. The delegates to the Constitutional Convention were aware of the historical applications of a federal form of government in ancient Greece and modern Switzerland, but the federal system for which they provided was not the result of a pre-existing political theory being written into law. It was, rather, the product of colonial practices under which local governments had been allowed considerable autonomy, and the political compromises at the convention between those delegates who wished to draft a charter for a unitary state and those who simply desired to improve the existing Articles of Confederation. The appropriate division of powers between those two levels was one of the major concerns of the founders.

THE FEDERAL POWER POSITION

A strong central government could only be created by taking powers away from the existing state governments and delegating them to the central government. Thus the United States is often referred to as a government of "delegated powers." The most significant listing of powers delegated to Congress is found in Article I, section 8, ranging all the way from the punishment of counterfeiting to the declaration of war. These specifically stated authorizations covered all the subjects which occurred to the founders as necessary for the new central government to possess. Moreover, the authorizations were typically stated very broadly, as for example the power to regulate commerce and to levy taxes.

Backing up these broad grants of specific powers, moreover, was the general authorization to Congress in the last clause of Article 1, section 8, "to make all laws which shall be necessary and proper for carrying into execution the foregoing powers. . . . " The relationship of clause 18 to the enumerated powers preceding it quickly became the subject of controversy between Federalists and Jeffersonians, between broad and strict constructionists. The issue was joined over Hamilton's plan for a national bank, as presented to the First Congress. There was no authorization in the Constitution for Congress to create a bank; in fact, the convention had specifically refused to grant to Congress even a restricted power to create corporations. On President Washington's invitation, Hamilton and Jefferson submitted their respective views on whether he should sign the bill, and their statements still stand as classical expositions of divergent theories of constitutional interpretation.

Jefferson emphasized the "necessary" in the necessary and proper clause. Since all the enumerated powers could be carried out without a bank, it was not necessary and consequently not authorized. Hamilton, on the other hand, argued that the powers granted to Congress included the right to employ "all the *means* requisite and fairly applicable to the attainment of the *ends* of such power," unless they were specifically forbidden or immoral or contrary to the "essential ends of political society." The Hamilton theory of a broad and liberal interpretation of congressional power was successful in persuading Washington to sign the bank bill, and it has generally predominated in subsequent constitutional development.

In 1819 Chief Justice John Marshall gave the definitive statement of this view in the great case of *McCulloch v. Maryland,* in which congressional authority to create a bank—the Bank of the United States, incorporated by statute in 1816—was again the issue. Marshall found implied congressional power to establish a bank in the expressly granted powers to collect taxes, to borrow money, to regulate commerce, to declare and conduct a war; for "it may with great reason be contended, that a government, entrusted with such ample powers, on the due execution of which the happiness and prosperity of the nation so vitally depends, must also be entrusted with ample means for their execution." A corporation was such a means. "It is never the end for which other powers are exercised."

Marshall analyzed the necessary and proper clause at length. He rejected the strict Jeffersonian interpretation, which "would abridge, and almost annihilate this useful and necessary right of the legislature to select the means." His final, and famous, conclusion was: "Let the end be legitimate, let it be within the scope of the constitution, and all means which are appropriate, which are plainly adapted to that end, which are not prohibited, but consistent with the letter and spirit of the constitution, are constitutional."

In considering the power position of Congress, it should also be noted that the Constitution made a few specific prohibitions on exercise of Federal power, such as suspending the writ of habeas corpus or levying direct taxes without enumeration. When the Bill of Rights was adopted in 1791, the extensive prohibitions of the first eight amendments were added to this group of restrictions on Federal power.

THE STATE POWER POSITION

In the Constitution as originally drafted no effort was made to state any general formula reserving to the states the powers not delegated to Congress. That nondelegated powers remained with the states was regarded as so obvious that it did not need to be spelled out. However, specific assurances were demanded during the ratification debates, which were met by adding the Tenth Amendment: "The powers not delegated to the United States by the Constitution, nor prohibited by it to the States, are reserved to the States respectively, or to the people."

The Tenth Amendment was clearly not intended to be a limitation on Federal powers, for it excepts from its effect "powers . . . delegated to the United States." Nevertheless, advocates of states' rights and antagonists of Federal authority have periodically attempted to create out of the Tenth Amendment barriers to Federal action authorized elsewhere in the Constitution. On the Supreme Court under Chief Justice Roger B. Taney, the doctrine of "dual federalism" asserted that the two levels of government were coequal sovereignties, and that authority delegated to the national government was limited by the powers reserved to the states in the Tenth Amendment.

The theory of dual federalism can be best illustrated by the Supreme Court's decision in *Hammer v. Dagenhart* (1918). Congress had passed in 1916 a statute forbidding the transportation in interstate commerce of goods produced by the labor of children below certain ages. This was clearly a regulation of commerce, and the Supreme Court had approved earlier statutes making use of this same power for other purposes. But in the *Hammer* case the Court majority asserted that the age at which children could go to work in factories was a local matter which had been reserved to the states under the Tenth Amendment. For the five-judge majority, Justice Day wrote: "The grant of authority over a purely federal matter was not intended to destroy the local power always existing and carefully reserved to the States in the Tenth Amendment." He went on to say that in interpreting the Constitution it should never be forgotten that "the powers not expressly delegated to the National Government are reserved" to the states and the people by the Tenth Amendment.

To arrive at this conclusion Justice Day had to misquote the amendment; the term "expressly" does not appear in its text. Indeed, when the Tenth Amendment was under consideration in the First Congress the anti-Federalists had tried to insert the word "expressly," but had been voted down. In any case, the commerce power had been expressly delegated to Congress. These errors did not go unchallenged. Speaking for the four dissenters Justice Oliver Wendell Holmes declared: "I should have thought that the most conspicuous decisions of this Court had made it clear that the power to regulate commerce and other constitutional powers could not be cut down or qualified by the fact that it might interfere with the carrying out of the domestic policy of any

State." Eventually, in 1941, the Supreme Court overruled the faulty majority opinion and established Holmes' position as the law of the Constitution.

THE SUPREME LAW OF THE LAND

The Constitution thus set up ground rules for the federal system by an allocation of authority to the two levels of government. But this was not enough. Conflicts over the division of functions were bound to occur between the states and the nation. To make the federal system work there needed to be rules for deciding such contests, and an umpire to apply those rules. The principal rule of this kind supplied by the Constitution is the "supremacy clause" of Article VI: "This Constitution, and the laws of the United States which shall be made in pursuance thereof; and all treaties made, or which shall be made, under the authority of the United States, shall be the supreme law of the land; and the judges in every state shall be bound thereby, any thing in the Constitution or laws of any state to the contrary notwithstanding."

The effectiveness of this section was early demonstrated in the case of *McCulloch v. Maryland* already mentioned. The specific issue here was the validity of a tax levied by the Maryland legislature on the federally chartered Bank of the United States. The cashier of the Baltimore branch of the Bank refused to pay the tax and was convicted of violating the law by the state courts. The Supreme Court unanimously upheld the Bank's position, Chief Justice Marshall basing his opinion squarely on the supremacy clause. "If any one proposition could command the universal assent of mankind," he wrote, "we might expect it would be this: that the government of the Union, though limited in its powers, is supreme within its sphere of action." Consequently, no state had any power "to retard, impede, burden, or in any manner control, the operations of the constitutional laws enacted by congress."

When Congress enters a field in which it is authorized to act, then, its legislation voids all incompatible state regulations. In practical terms, however, the question whether Congress has preempted a given area is a difficult one, since Federal statutes seldom state whether all local rules on the matter are suspended. It falls ultimately to the Supreme Court to determine the relation of Federal and state statutes.

In *Pennsylvania v. Nelson* (1956), Chief Justice Warren attempted to codify the tests which the Court has used to guide such decisions. First, is the scheme of Federal regulation so pervasive as to make it a reasonable inference that Congress has left no room for the states? Second, do the Federal statutes touch a field in which the interest of the national government is so dominant that it must be assumed to preclude state action on the same subject? Third, does enforcement of the state act present a serious danger of conflict with the administration of the Federal program?

In the *Nelson* case, a conviction for violation of the Pennsylvania sedition act had been reversed by the state supreme court on the ground that a Federal sedition act (the Smith Act of 1940) had occupied the field and superseded the state law. The United States Supreme Court agreed. Using the three criteria just suggested, Warren concluded that Congress had taken over the entire task of protecting the Federal government from seditious conduct when it passed the Smith Act, even though no express intention to exclude the states was stated in that statute.

THE UMPIRE

The umpire for deciding conflicts between state and nation over the constitutional division of functions is, as we have just seen, the Supreme Court. That the enforcement of the principle of Federal supremacy was essentially a judicial task was implied in the supremacy clause. The First Congress saw the necessity to spell out the Supreme Court's powers of review over the decisions of state courts so that the supremacy of the Federal Constitution could be preserved. The Judiciary Act of 1789, in section 25, provided for such review of final judgments or decrees in state courts in three classes of cases: (1) where the validity of a Federal law or treaty was "drawn in question," and the decision was against its validity; (2) where a state statute was questioned as "repugnant to the constitution, treaties or laws of the United States," and the decision was in favor of its validity; and (3) where the construction of the Federal Constitution, treaty, or statute was drawn in question, and the decision was against the title, right, privilege, or exemption claimed.

These categories were all based on the principle that if the Constitution and laws of the United States were to be observed, the Supreme Court would have to have an opportunity to review decisions of state courts which ruled adversely on asserted Federal rights. Courts in some states, particularly Virginia, did not submit without a struggle to the idea that their decisions were subject to review by the Supreme Court. However, the Supreme Court's authority was firmly asserted and established by two great early decisions, *Martin v. Hunter's Lessee* (1816) and *Cohens v. Virginia* (1821).

STATE RESISTANCE
TO FEDERAL AUTHORITY

The nature of the Federal union created by the Constitution was a perennial matter of controversy which finally led to a tragic civil war. The issue in 1861 was slavery, but earlier there had been several other controversies which had led to the elaboration of theories of state resistance to Federal authority.

One resulted from passage by a Federalist Congress of the Alien and Sedition Acts of 1798. These statutes were aimed at the opposition Jeffersonian party and at the partisans of France, many of whom were aliens. The laws enacted some harsh restrictions on aliens and punished criticism of the government. Jefferson and Madison, searching for a basis to attack these laws, drafted the so-called Virginia and Kentucky Resolutions and secured their adoption by the legislatures of these two states.

The doctrine of these resolutions sounded rather radical. In the Kentucky Resolutions Jefferson seemed to argue that the states had an "equal right" with the Federal government to interpret the Constitution, and that they could nullify acts passed by Congress which they deemed unauthorized. Madison in the Virgina Resolutions suggested that the states could "interpose" their authority to prevent the exercise by the Federal government of powers not granted by the Constitution.

This language about nullification and interposition sounds more threatening than Jefferson and Madison probably intended. Certainly they were deadly serious in their beliefs that the Federalist Congress had passed legislation prohibited by the Constitution, and in wanting to organize resistance to it. But both sets of resolutions were vague as to how such resistance was to be carried out. They certainly did not mean to assert that the Union was a system of fully sovereign states, a confederation from which each state could retire at any time. Jefferson's victory over the Federalists in the election of 1800, due in no small part to popular resentment over the Alien and Sedition Acts, terminated this cause of conflict.

A much more clearly elaborated theory of nullification and resistance to national authority was stated in 1828 by John C. Calhoun as a rationalization of Southern opposition to the continuous increase in tariff rates between 1816 and 1828. Calhoun was alarmed at the open talk of

secession in the South, and offered the doctrine of nullification as a sub-
stitute, contending that his plan was a logical extension of the Virginia
and Kentucky Resolutions.

Calhoun held that the Constitution was a compact formed by "sovereign and independent communities." The national government was not
a party to the compact but an emanation from it, "a joint commission,
appointed to superintend and administer the interests in which all are
jointly concerned, but having, beyond its proper sphere, no more power
than if it did not exist." He thought, however, that mere recognition of
the right of interposition would probably "supersede the necessity of its
exercise, by impressing on the movements of the Government that
moderation and justice so essential to harmony and peace, in a country
of such vast extent and diversity of interests as ours."

In 1832 South Carolina carried this theory to the point of action by
passing a statute purporting to nullify the Federal tariff acts of 1828 and
1832. President Jackson immediately challenged this action, saying that
the power of nullification was "incompatible with the existence of the
Union, contradicted expressly by the letter of the Constitution, unauthorized by its spirit, inconsistent with every principle on which it was
founded, and destructive of the great object for which it was formed."
He sent Federal vessels into Charleston Harbor to enforce the tariff, but
passage of a compromise tariff bill with lower rates made it possible for
South Carolina to withdraw its nullification statute.

The final test remained. In the years preceding the Civil War, with
the controversies over slavery and the tariff going on around them,
Southern statesmen shifted their ground from the right of nullification
to secession as a means to preserve their economic life and social
institutions. For Calhoun, secession was justified as a final remedy
to preserve states' rights. According to his theory, after a state had in-
terposed its authority to prevent Federal action, the Federal government could appeal to the amending process. If three-fourths of the
states upheld the Federal claim, the matter was settled as far as those
states were concerned. But the dissenting state was not obliged to
acquiesce in all instances.

> That a State, as a party to the constitutional compact,
> has the right to secede,—acting in the same capacity
> in which it ratified the constitution,—cannot, with
> any show of reason, be denied by any one who re-

gards the constitution as a compact,—if a power should be inserted by the amending power, which would radically change the character of the constitution, or the nature of the system.

Lincoln's decision to use force to keep the Southern states in the Union and the victory of the North in the Civil War closed the debate over the legality of secession. After the war, the Supreme Court tidied up a bit in *Texas v. White* (1869). The case hinged on the question whether or not Texas had ever left the Union, and the Court held:

> When, therefore, Texas became one of the United States, she entered into an indissoluble relation.... The act which consummated her admission into the Union was something more than a compact; it was the incorporation of a new member into the political body. And it was final. The union between Texas and the other States was as complete, as perpetual, and as indissoluble as the union between the original States.

Chief Justice Chase summed up the principle involved: "The Constitution, in all its provisions, looks to an indestructible Union, composed of indestructible States."

In 1956 the dust was blown off the doctrines of interposition and nullification, as they were invoked by several Southern states in protest against the Supreme Court's decision invalidating racial segregation in the schools. In its act of nullification the state of Alabama laid down the basic premise of its action:

> *Whereas* the states, being the parties to the constitutional compact, it follows of necessity that there can be no tribunal above their authority to decide, in the last resort, whether the compact made by them be violated; and, consequently, they must decide themselves, in the last resort, such questions as may be of sufficient magnitude to require their interposition.

Such assertions are of course in the plainest possible defiance of the history and principles of the federal system of the United States, and need only to be stated to reveal their falsity.

FEDERAL OBLIGATIONS TO THE STATES

Of the various obligations which the Constitution imposes on the Federal government with respect to the states, only one has actually involved significant Federal action. This is the responsibility of the United States to prevent domestic violence.

On application of a state legislature, or of the state executive, if the legislature cannot be convened, the United States must guarantee a state against "domestic violence" under Article IV, section 4. A request from the state legislature or governor is not necessary, however, where domestic violence threatens the enforcement of national laws. Article I, section 8, authorizes Congress to provide for calling forth the militia to execute the laws of the Union, suppress insurrection, and repel invasions. In 1792 Congress adopted legislation which, as revised in 1795, provided:

> That whenever the laws of the United States shall be opposed, or the execution thereof obstructed, in any state, by combinations too powerful to be suppressed by the ordinary course of judicial proceedings, or by the powers vested in the marshals by this act, it shall be lawful for the President of the United States, to call forth the militia of such state, or of any other state or states, as may be necessary to suppress such combinations, and to cause the laws to be duly executed. . . .

It was under this authority that President Eisenhower acted in 1957 when he sent Federal troops to control violence in Little Rock, Arkansas, and enforce Federal court orders seeking to accomplish gradual desegregation of the local high school. There were bitter protests from many quarters in the South against the President's action, but no judicial review of its validity was sought. President Eisenhower deplored the situation which had made it necessary to employ troops, but he said:

> When an obstruction of justice has been interposed or mob violence is permitted to exist so that it is impracticable to enforce the laws by the ordinary course of judicial proceedings, the obligation of the President under the Constitution and laws is inescapable. He is obliged to use whatever means may be required by the particular situation.

Other obligations of the Federal government toward the states are to maintain equal representation of the states in the Senate and to guarantee them a republican form of government. In 1912 the Supreme Court was asked to declare an Oregon system of direct legislation through the initiative and referendum to be a violation of a republican, i.e., representative, form of government. However, the Court ruled that the enforcement of this provision lay with the Congress.

INTERSTATE RELATIONS

The Constitution imposes certain obligations on the states in their relationships with each other. For one thing, they are required to extend the same privileges and immunities to citizens from other states that their own citizens enjoy. This means that out-of-state residents have the right to make contracts in the state, hold property, and have access to the courts, just as the state's own citizens. However, the interstate privileges and immunities clause (Article IV, section 2) does not preclude a state from treating citizens of other states differently when there are acceptable reasons why the two groups should be placed on different footings.

For example, the right to engage in normal businesses is protected, but the practice of such professions as medicine and law can be restricted to those licensed by the state. Similarly, a state can prevent persons coming from other states from voting until they have resided in the state for a certain period. Students from outside a state may be charged higher tuition in a state university than residents of the state.

Another obligation is that each state must accord full faith and credit to the public acts, records, and judicial proceedings of every other state. Consequently a court judgment rendered in one state can, if properly authenticated, be enforced in another state. Divorces granted in one state are generally recognized in all other states, although the lenient divorce laws in such states as Nevada and Florida have created some problems. In a 1945 case the Supreme Court held that North Carolina could refuse to recognize a Nevada divorce where it could be demonstrated that the parties, long-time residents of North Carolina, had never intended to establish a bona fide residence in Nevada.

The full faith and credit clause does not require a state to enforce the criminal laws of another state. The only obligation here is the provision requiring states to surrender fugitives from justice on the request of the governor of the state concerned. However, the Supreme Court has held that the Federal government cannot force a state official to take such action, and governors occasionally do refuse to honor a request for extradition.

THE POLITICS OF FEDERALISM

Whereas the constitutional arrangements thus far discussed provide the framework for operation of the Federal system, the actual activities of and relationships between the Federal and state governments at any particular period have been determined by the felt needs of the time, by popular demands and expectations as translated through the political process into governmental decisions. Looked at over the long reaches of United States history, there is an obvious trend toward increasing the powers and functions of the Federal government. Yet it is safe to say that Washington has never yet used all the powers it might justifiably claim under the Constitution, and there have been periods when the centralizing trend was reversed. The central-local relationship has been the product of political conflict, compromise, and consensus.

No detailed account of the politics of American federalism can be attempted here. Merely to follow the ebb and flow of centralizing trends through the major periods of our history is difficult. Of course the adoption of the Constitution was in itself a major victory of those forces favoring a strong national government, a victory which the Federalist party consolidated during the succeeding years under the astute guidance of Alexander Hamilton. But the anti-Federalist, states' rights forces were quickly rallied by Thomas Jefferson into a coalition strong enough to win the presidency in 1800 and ultimately to destroy the Federalist party itself. Once in office, however, Jefferson's Democrats by no means moved to dismantle the Federal establishment. In fact, Jefferson is particularly remembered for his bold move in purchasing the Louisiana Territory, in spite of his own expressed doubts about the constitutionality of such Federal action.

After the defeat of 1800, Federalist and nationalist ideology was kept alive by Chief Justice John Marshall on the Supreme Court. From 1801 to 1835 he devoted his immense judicial skill to broadening the constitutional interpretations of Federal power. His successor, Roger B. Taney, was of the opposite persuasion, and the years up to the Civil War saw the pendulum swing back toward state powers.

Out of the Civil War the Republican party emerged as the nationalist voice of the industrial East and Midwest, and the Democratic party as the states' rights spokesman of the South. But the responsibility of government which came to the Democratic party with Woodrow Wilson's election in 1912, and the necessities of wartime organization, laid the foundation for a reversal of party positions which was fully consolidated by Franklin D. Roosevelt's New Deal. From 1932 to 1952 the general Republican position was critical of the centralization attending the government's depression, war, and cold-war programs. In 1952 a Republican president took office pledged to reverse these centralizing tides. Although President Eisenhower did largely succeed in halting further increases in Federal functions, his efforts to find services which might be discontinued or returned to the states were almost completely without result.

What this experience suggests is that shifts of power toward the central government are not the result of political ideologies or conspiracies or Supreme Court decisions, but are rather caused by the inexorable pressures of wars, depressions, new means of communication, urbanization, industrialization, technology, and all the other factors which have shrunk the size of our world and created problems so large and so urgent that of necessity they are pushed up to the national level for handling.

This process of centralization has not required the granting of new constitutional powers to the Federal government. As will be developed more fully in the next chapter, such Federal authorizations as the commerce power and the taxing power have been fully adequate to support the greatly enlarged Federal establishment of the mid-twentieth century. For only one short period—from 1935 to 1937—did the Supreme Court construe the Constitution so narrowly as to threaten substantial Federal programs, but this crisis was soon past as the Court returned to long-established canons of broad construction of Federal powers. Particular programs of Federal centralization may be wise or unwise, but any program feasible enough politically to win the assent of Congress and the President is very unlikely to be lacking in satisfactory constitutional credentials.

COOPERATIVE FEDERALISM

Actually, it is highly misleading to talk about Federal centralization as though everything the Federal government does must be taken away from the states, or as though the only choice to be made is between Federal or state activity. In fact, a great many of the functions of our present Federal system are performed jointly by two or three levels of government. Nor is this a twentieth-century development. From the very beginnings of American federalism there has been more sharing of governmental functions than is commonly realized. Even before the Constitution was adopted, the Northwest Ordinance of 1787 gave grants-in-aid to the states for the support of public schools. Early examples of Federal-state administrative cooperation occurred in operation of the militia, law enforcement, court practices, conduct of elections, public health measures, pilot laws, and numerous other fields.

Today the list of cooperative Federal-state-local activities is almost endless. A dramatic example is in police work, in which the Federal Bureau of Investigation operates an active training program for state and local police officers, and assists them in crime solution with its fingerprint files and scientific detection laboratories. In the public health field Federal, state, and local programs are so intertwined that it may be difficult for an official to know in what capacity he is operating at a particular time. The national network of highways has been built up under a Federal-state cooperative program dating from 1916. The social security system, Selective Service, the National Guard— these and many other examples of cooperative federalism demonstrate how the levels of government work together.

Many of these joint efforts involve Federal grants-in-aid to the states. Originally Federal grants were of land, but in the twentieth century they have been grants of Federal funds. What are still called state "land-grant colleges" were originally established under the terms of the Morrill Act of 1862. Major grant-in-aid programs now cover the construction of highways and airports, vocational education and rehabilitation, social security programs, forest development, and school lunches.

The Federal government makes grants available to the states in order to promote activities regarded by Congress as beneficial to the public welfare, which the states might not undertake without Federal stimulus or support, or which they might be unable to undertake or to perform effectively except as part of a general program. One of the arguments often made for the grant-in-aid system is that Federal funds, which are distributed among the states according to a formula specified by Congress in each grant statute, can perform an equalizing function and enable the poorer states to bring their services up to an acceptable national minimum.

Another effect of the grant system has been to revitalize some areas of state activity and enable the states to retain certain activities which might otherwise have gone to the Federal government by default. When Federal grants are made available to the states, there are accompanying Federal regulations and requirements which ensure that state administration of the program will meet federally established standards. The states, of course, are also required to match the Federal funds in some degree.

The grant system has been attacked on the ground that it limits state discretion in the spending of funds, and forces the states to undertake activities which will bring in Federal money. It is also argued that grants from Washington merely return to the states tax receipts taken from them, and that this is unnecessary and costly centralization. However, there has been no decline in the use of the grant device, which has proved to be a useful method of achieving national purposes without direct Federal assumption of new functions.

States can also cooperate with each other in achieving common purposes. The Constitution authorizes interstate compacts, through the rather negative device of forbidding such compacts unless Congress consents to them. Interstate compacts have been employed to deal with such regional problems as conservation of natural resources, sharing of water in interstate streams, flood and pollution control, and regulation of interstate river basins or harbors. For example, the Port of New York Authority was set up by the states of New York and New Jersey to develop and operate harbor and transportation facilities in the bistate area. Compacts have not, however, proved very successful in achieving regulatory purposes.

The states have also joined in a program of promoting uniform state laws through a national conference, and they have sought to achieve more general cooperative purposes through the Council of State Governments, a central secretariat which provides research, publication, and information services for the states.

The Federal government has experimented with a regional approach to problems that concern more than one state but not the entire country. The most notable example is the Tennessee Valley Authority, established by Congress in 1933 to develop the resources of the Tennessee River basin. The TVA is headed by an independent three-man board based in the area and entirely outside the Washington bureaucracy. This organization has built up a highly efficient power system and encouraged regional developments which have substantially improved living standards in the area.

SUMMARY

Questions about the proper distribution of functions between the Federal government and the states will continue to arise. Centralization is fostered partly by the strength and unity of the national government, and partly by the disunity and weakness of the states. The national government has a strong and responsible executive, a representative Congress, and a reasonably efficient bureaucracy. In the states the governor's office is often too weak to provide leadership, the legislature is usually unrepresentative of the urban areas, and civil service too often does not attract able people.

Nevertheless, the states have an essential role to play in American federalism. Their status is firmly embedded in the composition of the Senate and in the major political parties, which at the national level are only coalitions of state organizations. The states are valuable laboratories in which new kinds of legislation can be tested. State boundaries may on occasion be barriers to the spread of misguided local political movements. Vigorous and dynamic state governments, alert to the needs of their citizens, can balance the Federal system and relieve the pressures on Washington. But no amount of preaching about states' rights will preserve those rights if the people who control state policy fail through neglect or shortsightedness to handle their own problems.

Review Questions

1. How did Hamilton and Jefferson disagree as to the powers of Congress?

2. What is the doctrine of dual federalism?

3. How are conflicts between Federal and state statutes handled?

4. What is the importance of the Supreme Court's power to review state court decisions?

5. What is the difference between the doctrines of interposition and nullification?

6. How can a state treat out-of-state residents differently from its own citizens without violating the interstate privileges and immunities clause?

7. What are the problems in according full faith and credit to Nevada divorces?

8. For what purposes have interstate compacts been used?

9. What are the advantages and disadvantages of Federal grants-in-aid to the states?

❦

CONGRESS AND FEDERAL POWERS

Chapter 3

The Constitution set up American governmental institutions on the separation of powers principle, and legislative, executive, and judicial functions are entrusted to three separate branches of government. The executive and the legislative are independent of each other in that they are each elected by separate electoral processes for assured terms of office. The President cannot dissolve Congress or shorten its term or remove any of its members. The Congress, even though it may have a majority which does not support the President, cannot remove him from office except by the difficult and politically dangerous process of impeachment. The Federal judiciary, although appointed by the President and confirmed by the Senate, is independent in the sense that it has tenure for life and its authority to enforce constitutional requirements on both the President and Congress is universally accepted.

Thus the term "separation of powers" has a degree of validity in describing the American system when contrasted with, for example, the English plan of concentrating authority in the legislature. The English executive is a council of ministers, headed by the Prime Minister, which is in effect a committee of the majority party in the House of Commons. The English judiciary has great prestige and security, but it cannot challenge the legitimacy of parliamentary action.

In many respects, however, "separation of powers" is a most misleading description of the American government. More accurately, the United States Constitution provides for a government of separated institutions sharing powers. The process of government requires that these separate institutions work together with some measure of effective cooperation, and this is perhaps the key problem of the constitutional system of the United States.

THE SEPARATED INSTITUTIONS

The institutional separation between Congress and the executive is exaggerated by their diverse electoral bases. The Senate is composed of two members from every state elected for six-year terms; it overrepresents the smaller states. In the House, a 435-man body whose members are apportioned to the states on the basis of population, the representatives are elected from congressional districts for two-year terms. The House represents local interests, particularly those of the rural areas which have more seats than they deserve on a population basis. The President, as will be discussed more fully in the next chapter, is chosen by an electoral system which gives disproportionate weight to the votes of the large industrial states. Thus each of these separated institutions has its own constituency.

Congress and the executive are, it is true, linked to some degree by a device for which the Constitution made no provision, the political party. However, there are many reasons why parties are of limited effectiveness in achieving cooperation between Congress and the President.[1] The main problem is that American national parties are federations of state and local organizations which join their efforts every

[1] For a fuller discussion, see *Politics and Voters* by Hugh A. Bone and Austin Ranney, in this series.

four years to nominate and elect a President, but which otherwise tend to go their separate ways. There is little national party discipline, and the members of Congress are more likely to win elections through attention to the interests of their state or district than through the help of the national party. Within each party there is a wide range of political views, and any President will find that a substantial number of his party's legislators disagree with his general policy position.

There are other factors limiting the effectiveness of party as a bridge between Congress and President. The electoral system does not guarantee that the President will have a majority of his own party in both houses of Congress, or even in one house. Though a President usually starts each four-year term with a majority in Congress, the mid-term legislative elections two years later customarily reduce his party's membership in Congress. President Eisenhower confronted Democratic majorities in both houses of Congress during six of his eight years in office.

Even when the President's party is in control of Congress, the legislative leadership may not be particularly hospitable to the President's views. The selection of House and Senate leaders is decided by the legislators themselves, and presidential interference in favor of his own candidates would be resented. Again, the chairmen of committees are selected strictly on the basis of seniority, which means that legislators unfriendly to the administration program may be in key congressional posts.

Separated by constitutional provisions on election and tenure, representing different constituencies of voters, and inadequately coordinated by party, the President and Congress are rivals for power and their characteristic relation is one of tension. This state is not a symptom of governmental failure. It is rather an indication that the system of separation of powers is operating normally. The Congress is too numerous and too poorly organized to originate a legislative program, or to assume leadership functions. This is the executive role. The President must tell Congress what he wants to have done. Congress, jealous of its autonomy, does not like to be told, and usually revises, delays, or ignores the President's program. But a President who knows his job will renew the pressure, using press conferences and television, patronage, and persuasion. The successful Presidents are those who do not take the separation of powers too seriously.

Congress possesses the power to impeach the President, or any other administrative or judicial official, though this process is too unwieldy to be of much practical importance. The impeachment procedure involves both houses of Congress, the House serving as the indicting body by voting impeachment charges. These charges are then tried before the Senate, where a two-thirds vote is necessary for conviction. The only President ever subjected to impeachment proceedings was Andrew Johnson in 1868, and the Senate failed by a margin of one vote to convict him. The defeat of that effort, which was motivated by vindictive partisanship, has fortunately discouraged subsequent use of impeachment as a weapon for political purposes.

LAWMAKING

The Constitution vests "all legislative powers herein granted" in the Congress. But lawmaking is one of the many "shared functions" in the constitutional system of the United States. The President is an indispensable participant, either by constitutional provision or by custom and necessity, in all stages of this process. In recent decades practically all important legislative proposals have originated in the executive. Article II, section 3, provides that the President "shall from time to time give to the Congress information of the state of the Union, and recommend to their consideration such measures as he shall judge necessary and expedient. . . ." Accordingly, the State of the Union message with a proposed legislative program is submitted by the President to Congress at the beginning of each regular session. It is followed by the President's budget message transmitting the executive expenditure recommendations for the following year, and the President's report on the state of the national economy as required by the Full Employment Act of 1946.

While Congress is in session the policy leadership of the administration is continuously manifested in the preparation of draft bills, testimony before congressional committees by department heads and other officials of the executive branch, and use of the President's vast powers as party leader and manipulator of public opinion. Under Article II, section 3, the President may even call Congress into special session to consider legislation he wants adopted, a power he has often used to bring added pressure on Congress.

All legislation must be submitted to the President for his signature before it becomes effective. Congress can override a presidential veto only by an extraordinary two-thirds majority in both houses. The President can permit a bill to become law without his signature by failing to sign and return it within 10 days after he has received it. This procedure is used when the President does not approve of a bill, but feels it impossible or impolitic to veto it. However, in these circumstances the bill will become law only if Congress is still in session after the 10 days have expired. If Congress adjourns within the 10-day period, the bill does not become law, and is said to have been given a "pocket veto."

The President must accept or reject a bill *in toto*; he has no power to veto items in a bill. Thus there is a temptation for Congress to attach legislation which the President is known to oppose, as a "rider" to some vitally important bill. Numerous proposals to give the President an "item veto" (i.e., the power to veto particular items without vetoing the entire bill), primarily with respect to appropriations measures, have uniformly failed.

In two particular fields of lawmaking—control of finances and departmental organization—Congress has gone far toward yielding its control to the President. The Budget and Accounting Act of 1921 established the principle and practice of the executive budget, under which the President is responsible for formulating and presenting to Congress a complete, detailed expenditure plan for the following fiscal year. Congress of course retains authority, in enacting the annual appropriation acts, to modify the executive budget in any way it sees fit. But as a practical matter, the congressional appropriations committees can give only a limited review to expenditure proposals totaling over 90 billion dollars annually.

The Congress, moreover, can merely authorize expenditures; it cannot compel the President to make them. Every President since Truman has differed on occasion with the Congress concerning national defense expenditures, and has placed in "reserves" and refused to spend money appropriated for certain military hardware. In 1962 such a controversy arose over a proposed new bomber. Secretary of Defense McNamara, arguing that manned bombers were being outmoded by missiles, wanted to spend comparatively little on this program. But Rep. Carl Vinson, chairman of the House Armed Services Committee, demanded that a large-scale program be undertaken, and his committee proposed legislation "directing" the President to spend this amount of money. Actually there would have been no way for Congress to enforce such a command, and the language was finally withdrawn on the promise of the Secretary to restudy the question.

Congress has power to pass laws setting up the Federal departments and agencies, but since 1933 it has largely delegated responsibility for

Federal reorganization to the President. A series of reorganization acts have authorized the President to prepare "reorganization plans" which may set up new departments or transfer bureaus or functions from one agency to another. These plans are submitted to Congress, and then go into effect automatically unless vetoed by either house of Congress within a specified time period. President Eisenhower created the Department of Health, Education and Welfare in this manner, but President Kennedy's reorganization plan establishing a Department of Urban Affairs was vetoed by the House in 1962.

INVESTIGATORY POWER

In an examination of the most significant legislative powers, the first to be noted is not even mentioned in the Constitution. The power of Congress to investigate is an implied power, supplementary to its specifically assigned functions to legislate, to appropriate, to pass on the elections and returns of members, and so on. It is an extremely broad power, because the need of Congress for information is broad, but at the same time it is not free from constitutional limitations.

In the famous case of *McGrain v. Daugherty* (1927), the Supreme Court upheld a Senate inquiry into Attorney General Harry M. Daugherty's conduct of the Department of Justice under President Harding. The Senate resolution had specifically directed a select committee to look into Daugherty's failure to prosecute the key figures of the Teapot Dome scandal as well as violators of the antitrust acts and other Federal statutes. In the course of its work the committee had occasion to subpoena Mally S. Daugherty, brother of the Attorney General. He failed to honor the subpoena and secured a writ of habeas corpus from a Federal district judge, who ruled that the Senate was exceeding its proper legislative powers in making this investigation, and was really conducting a trial of the Attorney General.

The Supreme Court, however, concluded that the committee was investigating the administration of the Justice Department, which was a subject "on which legislation could be had and would be materially aided by the information which the investigation was calculated to elicit." But the Court did point out that Congress had no "general" power to inquire into private affairs and compel disclosures, and that a witness "rightfully" might refuse to answer where the bounds of congressional power were exceeded or "the questions are not pertinent to the matter under inquiry."

The instrument through which Congress brings pressure on witnesses before its committees is the power to punish refusal to testify as contempt of Congress. Although Congress can itself try persons for contempt of its authority and imprison those found guilty, it has preferred to act through the courts. By an 1857 statute Congress provided that persons refusing to appear before a legislative committee or to answer questions pertinent to an inquiry should be deemed guilty of a misdemeanor and be subject to indictment and judicial punishment. Under this act there is full opportunity for reviewing courts to determine whether the legislative conclusion that contempt had been committed was justified.

The Communist-hunting activities of the House Committee on Un-American Activities, and Sen. Joseph McCarthy's activities in the Committee on Government Operations between 1950 and 1954, posed some difficult questions concerning the scope of the investigatory power. Many persons refused to answer inquiries by these committees on the ground that under the Fifth Amendment they could not be forced to give information that might be used against them in a criminal prosecution. This course guaranteed against a contempt citation, but laid the witness open to loss of employment and reputation, as witness Senator McCarthy's frequent charges about "Fifth Amendment Communists." Other witnesses refused to take refuge in the Fifth Amendment, and declined to answer on the claim that their rights to freedom of speech and opinion under the First Amendment were being infringed.

For a considerable period the Supreme Court avoided passing on the serious constitutional issues raised by these inquiries. Finally, in *Watkins v. United States* (1957), the Court did uphold a witness who had declined to testify before the Un-American Activities Committee, and indicated some intention to assume a measure of responsibility for determining whether congressional committees were operating within their constitutional authority.

Watkins was a labor union official who refused to answer questions as to whether certain individuals were members of the Communist Party. He agreed to testify concerning persons whom he believed to be active current Communists, but refused to answer questions concerning former members who to his best knowledge had long since removed themselves from the movement. He contended that such questions were not authorized by law or relevant to the work of the committee; answers would accomplish no purpose except exposure of past activities.

Chief Justice Warren's opinion for a divided Court pointed out that "there is no general authority to expose the private affairs of individuals without justification in terms of the functions of Congress," nor can a congressional committee act as a law enforcement or trial agency. Those are functions of the executive and judicial departments. However, the Chief Justice avoided any problem of testing the "motives" of committee members by transferring the argument to another ground—the vagueness of the investigatory mandate which the House had given to the Committee. Under its authorization to investigate "un-Americanism," the Committee could take up any subject it wished, and individuals could be compelled to testify about their beliefs, expressions, or associations in a way that deprived them of their First Amendment rights.

The *Watkins* decision was bitterly criticized as an infringement on congressional freedom to secure information, though in fact it resulted in no revision of the authority under which the Un-American Activities Committee operated, and little change in its procedures. Then, two years later, the Court by a 5 to 4 vote substantially reversed the *Watkins* holding in *Barenblatt v. United States* (1959). Here the Court minimized the vagueness of the mandate as an issue, and decided that the congressional concern for preservation of the country must override the First Amendment rights of individuals. Justice Harlan added that the Court could not look into the "motives" of congressional investigators. Justice Black for the four-judge minority held that this decision balanced away the rights of the First Amendment, and failed to see what was obvious in the whole history of the Un-American Activities Committee—namely, that its purpose was exposure and punishment, not the securing of information on which legislation could be based.

The same 5 to 4 support for the same Committee was expressed in two 1961 decisions, *Braden v. United States* and *Wilkinson v. United States*. This is a controversial area in which the Court's position may shift as new appointees come on the bench. But for the present the inclination of the Court is not to give judicial support to persons who defy congressional inquiries, provided the investigating committee is supported by a congressional authorization and gives the witness firm notice what it is investigating and why it wants his testimony. The Court is following the advice which Justice Jackson gave in 1949: "I should . . . leave the responsibility for the behavior of its committees squarely on the shoulders of Congress."

THE TAXING POWER

The broadest grant of fiscal authority to Congress is that in Article I, section 8, clause 1: "The Congress shall have power to lay and collect taxes, duties, imposts and excises, to pay the debts and provide for the common defence and general welfare of the United States. . . ." While this very broad grant of power is limited by some specific provisions, appearing elsewhere in Article I, the only restriction to give serious trouble has been the ban on "direct" taxes unless levied in proportion to population. The Federal income tax adopted by Congress in 1894 was held to be a direct tax and so unconstitutional. This decision delayed the inauguration of income taxation until 1913, when the Sixteenth Amendment was adopted.

Some additional limitations on Federal taxing power, though not specifically stated in the Constitution, have been announced and enforced by the Supreme Court. For one thing, Congress has often used the taxing power for purposes other than raising revenue. The best example is the protective tariff, which may impose customs duties so high as to keep particular foreign goods out of the country altogether. The purpose of such rates is not to bring in revenue, but to protect American manufacturers from foreign competition. The first tariff law was passed in 1789, but the Supreme Court never had occasion to rule on the constitutionality of this form of taxation until 1928. Then the Court upheld the tariff laws, saying: "So long as the motive of Congress and the effect of its legislative action are to secure revenue for the benefit of the general government, the existence of other motives in the selection of taxes can not invalidate Congressional action."

The Court has tended to use similar rationalizations to justify other tax statutes possessing obvious regulatory features. In 1866 Congress imposed a 10 per cent tax on notes issued by state banks, for the clear purpose of driving such notes out of circulation in favor of the notes of national banks. The Court upheld this action in 1869 on the ground that the taxing power was being used merely to aid the national government in its admitted power to establish a sound and uniform currency. An even more extreme use of Federal taxing power was a tax of 10 cents a pound on colored oleomargarine, while uncolored butter substitutes were taxed only ¼ cent per pound. This tax was obviously passed at the behest of the dairy interests, but the Court denied in *McCray v. United States* (1904) that "the motives or purposes of Congress are open to judicial inquiry in considering the power of that body."

There have been a few tax programs, however, in which the Court did find congressional nonrevenue motives too apparent to accept. One was the child labor tax, adopted in 1919 after the first child labor act, based on the commerce clause, had been held unconstitutional. The tax statute was clumsily drafted, and the Court found its regulatory purpose plainly visible on the face of the statute, with no need to go behind the act to prove that it was not a revenue measure. Similarly a grossly disproportional Federal excise tax, amounting to $1,000, imposed only on retail liquor dealers carrying on business in violation of local law, was declared unconstitutional.

A second limitation which the Court has read into the Federal taxing power is an immunity for the operations and activities of state and local governments. The immunity doctrine was first developed by the Court in *McCulloch v. Maryland* (1819), when it served to protect the Bank of the United States from state taxation. It was not until 1871 that this doctrine was applied in reverse to hold the salary of a state judge immune from the temporary Federal Civil War income tax. In 1895 the *Pollock* decision exempted from Federal taxation the interest on state and local bonds.

From this start, the conservative Court of the 1920s went on to extend tax immunity to a wide variety of state-connected activities. For example, a Federal tax on the income which private persons derived from leasing state-owned oil lands was invalidated by the Court. During the same period Federal immunity from state taxation was similarly expanded by the Court.

These exaggerated notions of intergovernmental tax immunity were eliminated by the more liberal Court of the late 1930s. Reciprocal exemption of both Federal and state employees from income taxation was terminated, and the oil-lands leasing cases were reversed. Tax exemption on income from state and municipal bonds remained as the principal limitation on congressional taxing power, and even this exemption probably no longer rests on a constitutional base.

SPENDING AND BORROWING

The language of Article I, section 8, authorizes Congress to levy taxes in order to "pay the debts and provide for the common defence and general welfare. . . ." This is spending authority of such expansiveness as to leave Congress substantially free from limitations on its appropriating power. The principal tests have occurred in connection with Federal grant-in-aid legislation under which Congress has made

Federal funds available to the states for financing programs which Congress wishes to promote.

The first important effort to invalidate such a Federal spending program came in *Massachusetts v. Mellon* (1923), involving the Maternity Act of 1921 which offered funds to the states for carrying on programs of health protection for mothers and infants. But this attack was frustrated by the Court's ruling that a lawsuit challenging the validity of a Federal spending program can be prosecuted only by a litigant who has a sufficient legal interest in Federal expenditures to give him standing to sue. Neither the state of Massachusetts nor an individual Federal income taxpayer had sufficient standing to entitle them to raise the issue, the Court held.

The case of *United States v. Butler* (1936), however, stands as an important exception to the rule that it is normally impossible to secure a court test of Federal spending power. The Agricultural Adjustment Act of 1933 had provided for Federal payments to farmers cooperating in the government's program of price stabilization through production control. The money paid the farmers was to come from processing taxes on agricultural commodities authorized by the same statute. This statutory joinder of a spending program with the tax arrangements for financing it was quite unusual, and gave the Court, which was at that time in a bitterly anti-New Deal mood, an opening which it quickly exploited. It held that the tax and the spending were in fact "parts of a single scheme" to regulate and control agricultural production, a field which belonged to the states. Consequently the act was unconstitutional under the Tenth Amendment.

The fear that the *Butler* principle might be applied against the tax provisions of the Social Security Act adopted in 1935 proved unfounded. *Steward Machine Co. v. Davis* (1937) involved the unemployment compensation provisions of the Act, which provided for a Federal tax on employers of a certain percentage of the wages they paid to employees. The proceeds of the tax went into the general Federal treasury. If employers paid into an unemployment fund set up under a satisfactory state law, they could credit such payments against the Federal tax up to 90 per cent.

The Supreme Court denied by a 5 to 4 vote that these tax provisions were an attempt to coerce the states or to invade their reserved powers. True enough, the states were given a compelling inducement to provide unemployment compensation, but the Court viewed this not as coercion but as freedom to adopt such social legislation without putting the employers of some states at a disadvantage compared with employers in states without unemployment compensation. The *Butler* case was specifically distinguished in the *Steward* decision on the grounds that here the proceeds of the tax were not earmarked for a special group; that the state itself had passed, and could at its pleasure repeal, the unemployment compensation law which was a condition of the credit; and that the relief of unemployment was an end for which nation and state could lawfully cooperate.

Congress has constitutionally unlimited power "to borrow money on the credit of the United States." There is no specific authority to issue paper money, and the "greenbacks" by which the Civil War was financed were first held unconstitutional in 1870 by a 4 to 3 vote of the Supreme Court. However, after two vacancies on the Court had been filled by President Grant, the Court reconsidered the issue and overruled the first decision by a vote of 5 to 4.

In 1933 the New Deal reduced the gold content of the dollar and nullified all provisions in private contracts and government bonds which called for payment in gold. The Supreme Court upheld this action as applied to private contracts, on the ground that individuals could not be allowed to frustrate the government's monetary program. The government itself could not, on the other hand, abrogate the promise to pay in gold coin, but the Court kept this holding from having any practical effect by adding that suit could be brought only for actual losses as a result of the government's action. Congress terminated the matter by passing a statute denying consent to sue the government on these grounds.

THE COMMERCE POWER

"The Congress shall have power," says Article I, section 8, clause 3, "to regulate commerce with foreign nations, and among the several states, and with the Indian tribes." The language is in terms of a positive grant of power to Congress, but in fact its purpose was also to take away from the states this power which they had so seriously abused to the detriment of the general commercial development under the Articles of Confederation. As it turned out, Congress was slow to utilize this grant of authority, and for the first century of national existence the primary problem in interpreting the commerce clause was to decide how much regulatory power remained with the states under the Constitution.

This was the issue presented in *Gibbons v. Ogden* (1824), the first commerce clause decision and one in which Chief Justice Marshall laid down principles that have affected all subsequent interpretations of the constitutional language. New York State had granted to certain interests a monopoly on steamboat transportation on waters within the state. The monopoly was challenged by Gibbons, who was operating a steamboat between New York and New Jersey under a license granted by the Federal government, and the Court struck down the New York monopoly on a finding of conflict between the state and Federal statutes.

In the course of the decision Marshall expressed the opinion that the congressional power over commerce "may very well be restricted to that commerce which concerns more states than one." Eventually this suggestion was developed into the distinction between "interstate" and "intrastate" commerce, and Federal power was limited to the former category.

Any operation which crosses a state line obviously falls in the "interstate" area. Thus interstate railroad, motor, aviation, pipeline, navigation, electric, or communications services are clearly subject to congressional control. Conversely, commercial operations which do not cross state lines have a prima facie claim to escape congressional regulation. This constitutional distinction came to be of great practical importance toward the end of the nineteenth century when Congress began to make important use of its regulatory powers by such laws as the Interstate Commerce Act and the Sherman Antitrust Act. Thus a prosecution of the sugar trust under the Sherman Act was defeated by the Supreme Court in 1895 on the ground that the refining of sugar took place in one state and was a completely separate process from its distribution in interstate commerce. "Commerce succeeds to manufacture, and is not a part of it," the Court said.

Over "commerce" as thus interpreted, however, the Supreme Court has approved complete exercise of congressional power to accomplish not only protection and promotion, but also restriction or even complete prohibition. In fact, Congress has on numerous occasions used the commerce power as a kind of national police power. A statute making it unlawful to transport lottery tickets from state to state was upheld by the Court in 1903, and the same device of exclusion from the channels of interstate commerce was later successfully used against impure food and drugs, and the white slave traffic.

Congress then sought to use this same method to attack child labor by statute in 1916, but the Court held the act unconstitutional by a 5 to 4 vote in the famous case of *Hammer v. Dagenhart* (1918). The Court tried to explain this inconsistency by arguing that lottery tickets and impure foods were harmful in and of themselves, whereas goods produced by child labor "are of themselves harmless." It was obvious from the beginning that this distinction was irrelevant to a determination of congressional power, and the decision was overruled by the Supreme Court in 1941.

The commerce concept has never depended entirely on the test of crossing a state line, however. After all, Marshall had talked about commerce that "concerns" more than one state, and commerce need not cross a state line to be of concern to other states or to the nation. The Supreme Court has long held that commercial transactions taking place entirely within a state may have such an effect on commerce among the states as to justify or require their regulation.

This "effect" doctrine has been applied in many situations. For example, where there is a "stream of commerce" moving across state lines, as in the raising of cattle and sending them off to stockyards to be slaughtered and prepared as meat products, or in the growing, transportation, and distribution of grain, sales in the stockyards or on the grain exchanges are integral parts of a stream of commerce which are subject to congressional regulation. Again, where intrastate freight rates provide unfair competition with goods moving under interstate rates, then Congress can control the intrastate rates.

The "effect" doctrine has the potentiality, if liberally interpreted, of extending congressional control to all commerce, for there is no commercial transaction which does not have some slight effect on the national economy. The Supreme Court was well aware of this possibility, and so it endeavored to provide some restrictions to keep the effect doctrine within bounds. The device developed for this purpose was the "direct-indirect" distinction. A direct effect on commerce could be the basis for Federal control, but an indirect effect could not. It was up to the Supreme Court, of course, to decide which effects were direct and which indirect.

Perhaps the two most noteworthy cases in which the Court denied Congress power to regulate because of this test were *Schechter Poultry Corp. v. United States* (1935) and *Carter v. Carter Coal Co.* (1936). Two important New Deal recovery statutes were invalidated by these decisions.

Under the National Recovery Act, codes of fair practice had been promulgated by the President fixing minimum wages and maximum hours, and regulating unfair or destructive competitive practices. In the *Schechter* case the live poultry code had been applied to a Brooklyn slaughtering plant which sold chickens to retail dealers in the vicinity. The Court unanimously held that these activities were not transactions in interstate commerce, nor could it find that they directly affected commerce. Chief Justice Hughes was not able to define the difference between direct and indirect effects, but he was sure that the distinction was "a fundamental one, essential to the maintenance of our constitutional system."

In the *Carter* case the Court majority similarly concluded that, although interstate commerce might be "greatly" affected by the ills which the coal code was attempting to remedy, it could never be "directly" affected. Coal production was a local activity. A production crisis in every part of the country simultaneously could never add up to a national problem with which Congress could deal.

A constitutional doctrine which held Congress powerless to alleviate national economic emergencies could not long be maintained. In 1937, in the landmark case of *National Labor Relations Board v. Jones & Laughlin Corp.*, the Court upheld the Wagner Act and in the process effectively terminated the "directness" test as a means of determining congressional power over commerce. In restoring what he called a "practical conception" of interstate commerce, Chief Justice Hughes did not overrule the *Schechter* and *Carter* opinions, but he said as little about them as was feasible. Speaking of the far-flung activities of this major steel company, he said:

> When industries organize themselves on a national scale, making their relation to interstate commerce the dominant factor in their activities, how can it be maintained that their industrial labor relations constitute a forbidden field into which Congress may not enter when it is necessary to protect interstate commerce from the paralyzing consequences of industrial war?

The *Jones & Laughlin* decision stated such a broad basis for the commerce power that few serious questions about the constitutional scope of congressional authority over commerce have subsequently arisen. The Fair Labor Standards Act, legislating minimum wages and maximum hours as conditions for the shipment of goods in interstate commerce, was upheld unanimously in 1941 in *United States v. Darby Lumber Co.*

Drastic agricultural regulations were accepted by the Court in

Wickard v. Filburn (1942). Here a farmer raising 23 acres of wheat, none of it intended for interstate commerce since all was to be consumed on the farm or fed to stock, was held to have such an effect on interstate commerce as to be liable to marketing quotas fixed under an act of 1938. The Sherman Act was held applicable to the insurance business in 1944, ending an immunity from Federal control which had been originally established by the Court in 1869. Professional baseball was given an obviously temporary exemption from congressional powers of regulation in *Toolson v. New York Yankees* (1953), but professional football, professional boxing, and the Shubert theatrical booking interests were all held subsequently to be interstate commerce and subject to the Sherman Act. As a result of the decisions since 1937, it is now clear that, in the words of Justice Cardozo, the commerce power of Congress is "as broad as the need that evokes it."

SUMMARY

From this review it is apparent that the Constitution gave Congress all the powers needed by a strong national government. The vast expansion of Federal activities in the twentieth century has been achieved with only one change in the Constitution—the adoption of the income tax amendment, which made possible the financing of government on its present scale. Even the barrier against the income tax was erected, not by the Constitution, but by a highly questionable Supreme Court decision. Similarly the Court in a few decisions misinterpreted the broad language of the commerce clause, and for a time in 1935 and 1936 threatened to hamstring legislative power over the national economy. But this threat quickly passed as the Court returned to Marshall's principles.

Congress has all the power it needs to deal effectively with space-age problems. If it has not always done so, the fault lies with legislative organization and leadership, matters not discussed in this volume.

Review Questions

1. Is "separation of powers" an accurate phrase for describing the American governmental system?

2. Why does Congress have such a wide range of functions?

3. What are the main problems in executive-legislative cooperation?

4. How does the impeachment process operate?

5. Why does Congress have the power to investigate when it is not mentioned in the Constitution?

6. Why has the Supreme Court seemed reluctant to limit the investigatory power of Congress?

7. Can Congress use its taxing power to achieve purposes other than the raising of revenue?

8. Why is it so difficult to test the constitutionality of congressional spending?

9. What tests of congressional power to regulate commerce has the Supreme Court employed?

10. Is "intrastate" commerce ever subject to congressional regulation?

THE PRESIDENT

Chapter 4

The establishment of a strong executive was one of the surprises of the Constitutional Convention. During the period immediately preceding the Revolution, the executive power, represented by the royal governors, had been far from popular, and when control passed into the hands of the states the first impulse was to slash away at the executive and exalt the legislatures. This same distrust of the executive was also present at Philadelphia in 1787, and proposals were heard that the executive branch be headed by a committee of three, for fear that a single official might develop monarchical powers. Again, it was argued that if a single executive was set up, he should be encumbered by a council.

These views were defeated by those who had seen the fumbling and the weakness of a headless government under the Articles of Confederation. Experience in the states had shown that an unchecked legislature could be as dangerous as a tyrannical executive ("The legislative department is everywhere extending the sphere of its activity," said Madison in 1787, "and drawing all power into its impetuous vortex"), and consequently a strong executive was favored to checkmate possible legislative usurpation. The office thus created has become the most important responsible executive on the globe.

THE EXECUTIVE ROLE

The President gets his tremendous authority from a variety of sources. Of course the basic authorizations are in the Constitution itself. Article II begins: "The executive power shall be vested in a President of the United States of America." It then continues with a number of more or less specific provisions, such as the power to grant pardons, to receive ambassadors, to make appointments, and to see that the laws are faithfully executed. But the actual use of executive power under these authorizations varies greatly with different incumbents of the Presidency. The language of Article II was the same under Buchanan and Coolidge as it was under Lincoln and Franklin D. Roosevelt, but the results were far different. The potentialities of leadership in the executive office which a strong man or perilous times can develop have been demonstrated time and again in American history.

In part the power of the American Presidency derives from the very character of the executive function, which John Locke referred to as "residual." Unlike the legislature, the executive is always in session, always capable of formulating a program and rousing opinion, and so always available to fill in gaps and meet emergencies. In the ultimate emergency of war, these executive qualities combine with the constitutionally delegated role of Commander in Chief to produce an office of almost unlimited power.

The President's executive position is greatly strengthened by the method of his selection. While there are complications to be examined shortly, he is in effect chosen directly by the entire American electorate, and he is the only elected official (other than the Vice President) who has the entire nation for his constituency and the consequent responsibility of speaking for the national interest. In addition the President is, by the fact of his election, the leader of his party—a source of great influence which the Constitution did not even contemplate.

Finally, the President is the ceremonial head of the nation, and his wife is the First Lady of the land. The good will which he may earn in performing his symbolic and nonpartisan duties can build up for him credit in the bank of public opinion on which he can draw in promoting his policy programs.

THE LIMITS OF EXECUTIVE POWER

With so many sources of authority on which he can rely, a resourceful President should have little difficulty in finding constitutional methods for achieving his purposes. The limitations on executive power which Presidents encounter are rarely the boundaries of the Constitution, but rather the confines of political feasibility. As suggested in the preceding chapter, the President is under the constant pressure of Congress which by the rules of the game must be suspicious of, if not hostile toward, many executive proposals or actions. Where joint action is required by the Constitution, the President is limited to what he can persuade Congress to accept.

The Federal judiciary is much less significant than Congress as a check on executive power. The Supreme Court concluded quite early in our history that it should not attempt to issue orders to the President. However, cabinet members and other subordinates are subject to judicial process, and administrative officers who are performing allegedly unconstitutional actions can be enjoined by the courts.

Where constitutional controversies about executive power have reached the courts, they have often been memorable conflicts. Perhaps the most important issue has been the latitude which the President may claim in meeting crises calling for the use of powers not specified in the Constitution. Is the President able to exercise "inherent" powers under emergency conditions?

In general, there have been two views on this subject. One is well summarized in the "stewardship" conception of the presidential office asserted by Theodore Roosevelt. In his *Autobiography* he set forth his belief "that it was not only his right but his duty to do anything that the needs of the Nation demanded unless such action was forbidden by the Constitution or by the laws."

On the other hand, William Howard Taft took a much more cautious and limited view of the President's powers. The President's proper role was faithfully to execute the *laws*, not his own conception of the national needs. In lectures which he gave in 1916 after his presidential term, he said:

> The true view of the Executive function is, as I
> conceive it, that the President can exercise no power
> which cannot be fairly and reasonably traced to
> some specific grant of power or justly implied and
> included within such express grant as proper and
> necessary to its exercise. . . . There is no undefined
> residuum of power which he can exercise because
> it seems to him to be in the public interest.

The Supreme Court has on occasion given support to both of these
positions. In several historic cases it has supported the use of broad
executive power to meet emergencies. At the time of the great Pullman
railway strike in 1894, for example, President Cleveland sent troops
to Chicago to keep the trains running, and had his Attorney General
secure a Federal court injunction against the strikers. There was no
explicit statutory basis for the injunction, but the Court sustained it
on the broad ground that the right of self-preservation must belong to
a government, whether claimed by statute or not, and that the executive was constitutionally entitled to act in such cases.

On the other hand, the Supreme Court in the 1952 *Steel Seizure* case
rebuked the action of President Truman in taking over the steel mills
to prevent a strike which would have interrupted the production of
munitions for American troops in Korea. There was no law of Congress authorizing this seizure. More important, Congress had in 1947
actually considered giving the President seizure power for such emergencies, and decided against it. Instead, Congress adopted the Taft-
Hartley provision authorizing the President to get a court injunction
imposing an 80-day "cooling off" period when such strikes were
threatened. The Court majority thought that in these circumstances
the President was obligated to use the remedy Congress had provided,
though Chief Justice Vinson and two other dissenting justices charged
that the Court was imposing a "messenger boy" concept on the
President.

Obviously there is little danger that the Supreme Court can turn the
President into a messenger boy. Ten years after the *Steel Seizure* decision another President was confronted with another steel problem.
President Kennedy had used the persuasive powers of his office to get
steel management and labor to sign a moderate new labor contract
which would not have an inflationary effect on the economy. But no
sooner was the contract signed than United States Steel announced a

price increase. President Kennedy, very angry at what he regarded as a deliberate flouting of his stabilization efforts, blasted the steel industrialists in a press conference and turned loose a series of moves including grand jury investigations of possible antitrust violations and proposals for new restrictive legislation, with the result that the price increase was withdrawn in three days. The steel price affair of 1962 affords a much more realistic index to presidential power than the *Steel Seizure* decision of 1952.

APPOINTMENT AND REMOVAL

The President's ability to control the executive branch rests primarily on his power to appoint—and if necessary to remove—all the higher policy-making officials. The appointing power is firmly grounded in Article II, section 2, but it is vulnerable in one respect—the requirement of senatorial confirmation for all appointees except "inferior officers." Thus the Senate has a veto power on appointments, and it is made more effective by the practice of "senatorial courtesy," which demands that appointees be personally acceptable to the administration senator or senators from the state where the appointee lives.

As for removal, impeachment is the only method mentioned in the Constitution. There is no language pertaining to the President's power to remove, or declaring whether officers appointed with the confirmation of the Senate can be removed by the President without Senate approval. However, the President's sole control of the removal power was practically unquestioned until after the Civil War. Then, in the bitter feud between Congress and President Johnson, Congress sought to capture a share in the removal power. The tenure of office act passed in 1867 denied the President's right to remove the heads of executive departments without the advice and consent of the Senate. A violation of this act, which Johnson contended was unconstitutional, was one of the charges on which he was impeached. The act was repealed in 1887 without any Supreme Court ruling on its validity.

In 1876 Congress passed an act providing for Senate participation in the removal of postmasters. Litigation under this statute finally resulted in a long-delayed vindication of Johnson's position in the case of *Myers v. United States* (1926). Myers, a postmaster in Portland, Oregon, was removed by President Wilson before the expiration of his four-year term without securing Senate consent. Myers sued for his salary for the remainder of his term, but the Supreme Court denied his claim on the ground that the 1876 act was unconstitutional.

Chief Justice Taft, who knew what the presidency looked like from the inside, and how important the removal power was, wrote the Court's opinion. He relied upon historical practice and also on the constitutional provisions vesting "executive power" in the President and charging him with faithful execution of the laws. From these responsibilities, Taft concluded:

> The reasonable implication, even in the absence of express words, was that as part of his executive power he should select those who were to act for him under his direction in the execution of the laws. The further implication must be, in the absence of any express limitation respecting removals, that as his selection of administrative officers is essential to the execution of the laws by him, so must be his power of removing those for whom he cannot continue to be responsible.

Though this decision could apply only to the type of position actually involved, Taft went on to assert that the principle of sole presidential responsibility would apply to all officers, even those to whom Congress had given "duties of a quasi judicial character . . . and members of executive tribunals." Nine years later the Supreme Court had to pass on a case of precisely this character when a member of the Federal Trade Commission was removed by President Roosevelt without any showing of cause, although the statute specified "inefficiency, neglect of duty, or malfeasance in office" as grounds for presidential removal. In *Humphrey's Executor v. United States* (1935) the Court unanimously held this language to be a valid restriction on the removal power.

Justice Sutherland, writing the Court's opinion, pointed out that the officer involved in the *Myers* case, a postmaster, was "restricted to the performance of executive functions," and rather lowly ones at that. In contrast, Humphrey was a member of "an administrative body created by Congress to carry into effect legislative policies embodied in the statute," performing its duties "without executive leave." The Federal Trade Commission is a "quasi-legislative or "quasi-judicial" agency, which Congress intended to discharge its duties "independently of executive control." Forbidding the President to remove its commissioners except for cause is a legitimate way of implementing that policy, "for it is quite evident that one who holds his office only during the pleasure of another, cannot be depended upon to maintain an attitude of independence against the latter's will."

It was rather generally thought from the *Humphrey* decision that the Court would require Congress actually to express by legislation its intention to limit the President's removal power before such limitation would be judicially recognized. However, in *Wiener v. United States* (1958), the Court extended the *Humphrey* principle to cover a quasi-judicial officer where there had been no specific statutory language protecting against removal. Under the *Wiener* decision, then, the President's power of removal, which normally can be exercised at his discretion, may be used against quasi-judicial officers only for cause.

FOREIGN RELATIONS

The provisions of the Constitution pertaining to foreign relations take the form of assignments of particular functions to the various branches of the government. They do not by any means cover the whole range of foreign affairs, and there is no grant of authority over foreign relations in broad terms comparable with the authorization to regulate commerce among the states and with foreign nations. However, such a grant is not necessary. Authority over foreign affairs is an inherent power, which attaches automatically to the Federal government as a sovereign entity, and derives from the Constitution only as the Constitution is the creator of that sovereign entity.

The principal theoretical writers on whom the founders relied—Blackstone, Locke, Montesquieu—were unanimous in contending that the power to carry on foreign relations must be vested in the executive. Nevertheless, the Constitution allocated the power to declare war to Congress. It made the Senate's consent necessary to the ratification of treaties, and by a two-thirds vote. It made the Senate's advice and consent a condition to the appointment of ambassadors. When account is taken of the general lawmaking and appropriating powers of Congress, the exercise of which is often essential to the formulation and execution of foreign policy decisions, it is clear that "the Constitution, considered only for its affirmative grants of powers capable of affecting the issues, is an invitation to struggle for the privilege of directing American foreign policy."[1]

For this struggle the President is powerfully equipped by the general

[1] Edward S. Corwin, *The President: Office and Powers*, New York University Press, New York, 1957, p. 171.

characteristics of executive power already noted, by his constitutional authority as Commander in Chief, and by his recognized position as "the Nation's organ for foreign affairs," to quote a phrase first used by John Marshall. The powers which the President exercises as "sole organ" can be briefly indicated.

He is the channel for communications to and from other nations, and conducts negotiations directly or through his appointed representatives. He has the power of recognizing foreign governments. He can use his control of the armed forces to implement his policies and to protect American rights or interests abroad. To a considerable degree these powers cancel out the most important grant of external authority to Congress, the power to declare war. For the President can, by his management of foreign affairs and his use of the armed forces, so shape the nation's policy and the development of events as to leave Congress no choice but to declare war.

On the other hand, the necessity of securing Senate consent by a two-thirds vote for the ratification of treaties has proved in practice to be a real limitation on executive policy making. The shambles which Senate obduracy has often made of United States foreign policy has led many students to conclude that consent to treaty ratification by a majority vote of the two houses of Congress would be preferable to the present arrangement.

Partly because of the hazards of Senate treaty approval, the President has made extensive use of "executive agreements" with foreign countries, which do not require Senate assent. They may be employed for minor matters which it would be inappropriate to embody in a treaty, but often they deal with matters of major importance. Unless such agreements are based on acts of Congress authorizing them, they are usually said to find their constitutional authority in the President's power as Commander in Chief or in his position as the sole organ of international relations. Efforts to distinguish between the legal effects of treaties and executive agreements have generally been unsuccessful.

Article VI sets up treaties and acts of Congress on a par—both are "the supreme law of the land." In case of conflict between a treaty and a statute, the later in point of time generally supersedes the earlier.

According to Article VI, laws must be made "in pursuance" of the Constitution in order to have status as supreme law of the land, but treaties need only be made "under the authority of the United States." Considerable effort has been made to conjure up from this difference in wording the bogey of a treaty power unlimited by the Constitution.

Some substance may seem to be given these fears by the fact that the Supreme Court has never held a treaty unconstitutional, and by the circumstances of the Court's decision in *Missouri v. Holland* (1920). There the Court held that a treaty entered into with Canada for the control of the shooting of wild game gave Congress power to adopt a regulatory statute in this area which it would have had no authority to pass in the absence of the treaty.

Admittedly this was a somewhat startling holding, but it was the inevitable consequence of the plenary nature of Federal power over foreign affairs. The complete incapacity of the states for foreign relationships requires that the Federal government have authority to deal with all matters which are of legitimate concern to American foreign relations. This does not mean, however, that the treaty power can be used to amend the Constitution, nor does it open up all constitutional rights to revision by treaties.

During the 1950s, American isolationists sought to raise doubt on these points as part of the campaign to secure adoption of the Bricker Amendment. The first section of the amendment, in its 1953 version, read: "A provision of a treaty which conflicts with this Constitution shall not be of any force or effect." However, this was clearly already the law on the subject. Any doubt on this score was removed in 1957 when the Court specifically held in *Reid v. Covert* that Article VI did not permit the United States "to exercise power under an international agreement without observing constitutional prohibitions."

COMMANDER IN CHIEF

In time of war the President's tremendous executive authority is even further expanded by his status as Commander in Chief. In No. 69 of *The Federalist*, Hamilton thought that the President's role as Commander in Chief would amount "to nothing more than the supreme command and direction of the military and naval forces, as first general and admiral of the Confederacy," while the more significant powers of declaring war and raising and regulating fleets and armies would be exercised by Congress. Actually this was an accurate enough forecast of the limited role of the Commander in Chief from 1789 to 1861. It was President Lincoln who, in his resolve to save the Union, linked together the presidential power to take care that the laws be faithfully executed with that of Commander in Chief to yield a result approaching constitutional dictatorship.

For 10 weeks after the fall of Fort Sumter until he called Congress into special session, Lincoln met the emergency by a series of actions which were for the most part without statutory authorization, though they were subsequently ratified by Congress. He added 40,000 men to the Army and Navy, closed the Post Office to treasonable correspondence, paid out 2 million dollars from unappropriated funds in the Treasury, proclaimed a blockade of Southern ports, suspended the writ of habeas corpus in several areas, and caused the arrest and military detention of persons suspected of treasonable practices. World Wars I and II, with their progressively greater impact on the civilian economy of the country, saw a proportionate increase in the President's wartime powers, though the expansion was achieved in nearly all cases with greater regard for the constitutional proprieties than was characteristic of the Civil War.

Lincoln's suspension of the writ of habeas corpus led to one of the great decisions in this field, *Ex parte Milligan* (1866). In a proclamation of September, 1862, Lincoln suspended the writ and ordered that all persons "guilty of any disloyal practice affording aid and comfort to the rebels" should be liable to trial by military commissions. Milligan was arrested at his home in Indiana late in 1864, tried by a military commission, and sentenced to be hanged. In May, 1865, he secured a writ of habeas corpus from the Federal court in Indianapolis, and a year later the Supreme Court ruled unanimously that the President had no power to order trial of civilians by military courts in areas where the regular courts were open and operating.

There was a considerable similarity between Lincoln's military commissions and the situation which prevailed in Hawaii during the greater part of World War II. Martial law was declared by the Governor of Hawaii immediately after the Japanese attack on December 7, 1941, and the President approved his action two days later. Civil and criminal courts were forbidden to try cases, and military tribunals replaced them during most of the duration of the war. In 1946, well after the end of hostilities, the Supreme Court held in *Duncan v. Kahanamoku* that when Congress in the Hawaii Organic Act had granted the governor power to declare martial law it had not meant to supersede constitutional guarantees of a fair trial by civil courts which apply elsewhere in the United States.

One of the most criticized of all executive wartime actions was the compulsory evacuation of persons of Japanese descent, most of whom were American citizens, from the West Coast after the beginning of World War II. The evacuation, first ordered in February, 1942, was shortly thereafter ratified by Congress, and the Supreme Court had to consider whether it would oppose the joint judgment of the President and Congress that this harsh action was required by military necessity. In *Korematsu v. United States* (1944), the constitutionality of the evacuation program was upheld on the ground that the military authorities were not unjustified in concluding that the Japanese residents of the Coast area constituted a potentially grave danger to the public safety, a danger so great and pressing that there was no time to set up procedures for determining the loyalty or disloyalty of individual Japanese.

Actually the Court made no effort to use that valuable prerogative of judicial review, the "wisdom of hindsight," to challenge the military conclusions, though it certainly was apparent by the end of 1944 that the fears of sabotage and treachery by West Coast residents of Japanese descent were entirely groundless. Only Justice Murphy charged that the case made by the military had not been based on any demonstrated public necessity, but upon "an accumulation of such of the misinformation, half-truths and insinuations that for years have been directed against the Japanese Americans by people with racial and economic prejudices."

ELECTION

The original method of selecting the President called for each state to "appoint, in such manner as the legislature thereof may direct, a number of electors, equal to the whole number of Senators and Representatives to which the State may be entitled in the Congress. . . ." The electors were to "meet in their respective States, and vote by ballot for two persons, of whom one at least shall not be an inhabitant of the same State with themselves."

The results of the vote were to be transmitted to the President of the Senate, who would open the sealed certificates in the presence of both houses, and the votes would then be counted. The person with the greatest number of votes was to be the President, provided he had a majority of the whole number of electors. If two candidates were tied, and both had more than a majority, the House was immediately to choose between them. If no candidate had a majority, then the House would choose from the five highest on the list. In either event the House was to vote by states, "the representation from each State having one vote," and a majority was required to elect. After the choice of President, the person having the next greatest number of votes was to be Vice President, and in the event of a tie, the Senate was to choose between the contenders.

This arrangement proved faulty very quickly. After Washington's two terms, the two newly developed political parties took over the task of choosing the electors, who then ceased to have any will of their own. The 1796 balloting gave the Presidency and Vice Presidency to different parties, John Adams and Thomas Jefferson ranking first and second in the electoral voting. In 1800 a tie resulted because Jefferson and Aaron Burr, the Republican candidates for President and Vice President, were voted for by each Republican elector. Everyone understood that Jefferson was the presidential choice, but the tie threw the election into the House, where it took all Hamilton's efforts to dissuade the lame-duck Federalists from giving the post to Burr.

This experience led to adoption of the Twelfth Amendment in 1804, and it still controls the electoral process. It made the following changes: (1) the electors were to ballot separately for President and Vice President; (2) if no candidate for President received a majority, the House, voting as before by states, was to choose "from the persons having the highest numbers not exceeding three on the list"; (3) the Vice President also had to receive a majority of the electoral votes, and if no one achieved a majority, the Senate was to choose between the two highest candidates; and (4) if the choice of President fell to the House, and it had not made a choice by March 4, the Vice President was to act as President.

This system has weathered two great crises, has three times been responsible for electing a President who had fewer popular votes than his leading opponent, and has been the cause of constant criticism. In 1824 there was no majority in the electoral college, and the House chose John Quincy Adams, though Andrew Jackson had a larger electoral and popular vote. In 1876 there was a dispute over 20 electoral votes, and Congress ultimately set up a completely extraconstitutional electoral commission to decide which votes to accept. This body, with an 8 to 7 Republican majority, decided in favor of the Republican electors and Hayes, with a popular vote minority, was elected by one electoral vote. In 1888 Harrison was the winner in the electoral college, though receiving 100,000 fewer popular votes than Cleveland.

Normally the electoral vote magnifies the popular vote margin of the winning candidate, largely because each state casts its entire block of electoral votes for the winner in that state. Other factors in distortion of the popular vote by the electoral result are the overweighting of the less populous states in the electoral college, and the varying rate of voter turnout in different states.

Another feature of the present system is that electors may refuse to cast their ballots in accordance with the results of the balloting in their state. In the elections of 1948, 1956, and 1960, one elector on each occasion failed to vote for the candidates of the party which he represented. Moreover, in 1960 eight "unpledged" electors from Mississippi and six from Alabama were elected in a throwback to the original electoral plan which challenged the principle of direct election.

Three main proposals for reform of the electoral system have been made. The first, simplest and most drastic, would require the President to be chosen in a direct nationwide popular election. This plan would terminate the advantages in overweighting of electoral votes which the smaller states now possess, and consequently the chance of securing ratification by three-fourths of the states of a constitutional amendment making this change appears remote.

A second proposal would retain the existing electoral vote distribution, but have electors chosen from the congressional districts. However, the two electors to which each state is entitled by reason of its two senators would continue to be chosen on the basis of the statewide popular vote.

The third proposal would also continue to assign electoral votes as at present (though the electors would be abolished), but the electoral vote of each state would be divided exactly in proportion to the popular vote each candidate received in the state, percentages being carried three places beyond the decimal point.

The sponsors of both the proportional and the district plans make much the same case against the present electoral system. They hope to broaden the base for selection of presidential and vice presidential candidates by decreasing the premium on nominees from the pivotal states. They want to reduce the excessive campaign importance of large, doubtful states. They wish to check the political power of large cities and especially of key minority groups within those cities. They desire to limit to some degree the currently excessive potential effects of local frauds, bad weather, intense local issues, and other accidental circumstances on the determination of electoral votes. They hope to increase the likelihood of a more widespread two-party system throughout the country.

On the other hand, it should be pointed out that reducing the electoral importance of the large states with their metropolitan centers would automatically enhance the power of the rural areas which are already overrepresented in the Senate and House. Moreover, under a proportionate plan the one-party states, which are predominantly rural or Southern or both, would have much greater influence. Thus a proportionate plan would merely create new imbalances in place of the old ones.

On behalf of the present system, it can be said that it has produced chief executives comparable in quality, if not generally superior, to those of other democratic nations. It has met crises successfully. It has made the Presidency a strong nationalizing force offsetting the localism and divisive characteristics of Congress. It has been a strong source of support for the two-party system, blocking development of third parties and the election of minority Presidents.

SUCCESSION

The language of Article II, section 1, on succession to the Presidency was not entirely clear, but constitutional practice has now determined its meaning. The provision is: "In case of the removal of the President from office, or of his death, resignation, or inability to discharge the powers and duties of the said office, the same shall devolve on the Vice President. . . ." It is not clear from this wording whether it is the "office" of President which devolves on the Vice President, or only the "powers and duties" of the office. If the latter is the intention, then the Vice President would become only an acting President. However, John Tyler, the first Vice President to face this problem, asserted his claim to full presidential status after the death of President Harrison in 1841, and this precedent has been fully accepted.

The Constitution authorizes Congress to declare what "officer shall . . . act as President" in case neither the President nor Vice President is living or able to serve. Congress in 1792 provided that the succession would pass first to the President pro tempore of the Senate and then to the Speaker of the House. It also required immediate steps to be taken for choosing a new President through the electoral college for a regular four-year term.

In 1886 Congress adopted a different theory of presidential succession, providing that the heads of the seven Cabinet departments then existing, beginning with the Secretary of State, should constitute the line of succession after the Vice President. This act repealed the 1792 provision requiring immediate election of a new President.

No use ever had to be made of either statutory plan. In 1947 Congress adopted still another succession act. Under this act the Speaker of the House is to act as President when a successor is needed, but he must first resign as Speaker. If there is no Speaker, the President pro tempore of the Senate, on resigning his post, is to act as President. In either case the acting President serves for the remainder of the current four-year term. Cabinet officers follow in the line of succession according to the seniority of their departments. The 1947 act has been subjected to much criticism as a less satisfactory solution than the 1886 act which it replaced.

PRESIDENTIAL INABILITY

The Constitution contemplates the necessity of carrying on the work of the Presidency in event of the incumbent's "inability to discharge the powers and duties" of the office through illness or for any other reason. It seems clear that the Constitution intended to permit the Vice President to act as President temporarily in such emergencies, the actual President resuming his post when the emergency was terminated. However, there has been enough fear of constitutional complications from having two Presidents at the same time to prevent any use of this authorization on occasions when it might have been appropriate.

President Eisenhower had three serious illnesses in a little over two years. Each of these emergencies created a temporary power vacuum, which could have been eased by having the Vice President become acting President for a temporary period. In the absence of any legislation or constitutional consensus on this problem, President Eisenhower in March, 1958, made public an agreement he had reached with Vice President Nixon concerning a possible future inability. This agreement called for the Vice President to serve as "acting President, exercising the powers and duties of the office until the inability had ended." Then the President "would resume the full exercise of the powers and duties of the office." President Kennedy entered into a similar agreement with Vice President Johnson in 1961.

SUMMARY

The American Presidency has been one of the great successes of the Constitution. The office has combined power with responsibility, action with deliberation. The system of electing the President is in some respects a historical relic, and the possibilities for malfunctioning in the electoral college are very real. In fact, however, the system has worked, and the President's obligation to a national electorate has been a great unifying force countering the divisive and parochial interests represented in Congress.

Executive powers are stated broadly in the Constitution, which is fortunate, because policy leadership can come only from the executive. Congress can counsel or ratify or restrain or nullify, but it cannot lead. The Supreme Court can reverse a specific executive act, such as the seizure of the steel mills, but the great mass of presidential actions are subject only to the control of executive wisdom and judgment, exercised in the setting of democratic discussion and criticism by an informed public opinion.

Review Questions

1. What were the difficulties with the original constitutional provisions for election of the President?

2. What are the main proposals now being discussed for revising the system of electing the President?

3. What have been the problems in establishing succession to the Presidency beyond the Vice President?

4. Why has the Vice President never become acting President during periods when the President is disabled?

5. Contrast the views of President Theodore Roosevelt and President Taft on presidential powers.

6. Did the Supreme Court in the *Steel Seizure* case hold that the President had no inherent executive powers?

7. What limitations can Congress impose on the President's removal power?

8. What are the powers which the President possesses for the control of American foreign relations?

9. What is the difference between treaties and executive agreements?

10. What was the Supreme Court's problem in determining the constitutionality of the wartime evacuation of Japanese from the United States West Coast?

❦

THE FEDERAL JUDICIARY

Chapter 5

The Supreme Court, one of the most distinguished and influential of the world's judicial tribunals, traces its position at the apex of the American judicial system directly to Article III of the Constitution. The members of the Constitutional Convention were clear that there had to be a top-level Federal court, but they were less certain whether Federal courts "inferior" to the Supreme Court were needed.

It was argued by some that the state courts could be authorized to try Federal cases, subject to review by the Federal Supreme Court. Others contended that the Constitution should provide for a full

Federal court system. The final decision was to hand this problem of Federal organization to Congress, and in the Judiciary Act of 1789 the advocates of a complete and separate system of Federal courts were successful.

ORGANIZATION

The Federal judicial system consists of three levels. There are 91 district courts, at least one in each state, and more than 300 district judges. Trials are held in the district courts before a single judge, except that when the constitutionality of a Federal statute is questioned, and in certain other situations, three judges must sit in trial of a case. At the intermediate level are the courts of appeals for each of the 10 circuits and the District of Columbia, with a total of some 80 judges. Each appeal is heard by a panel of three or more judges. Decisions of the courts of appeals may go for review to the Supreme Court.

The Federal judicial establishment also includes such specialized tribunals as the Court of Claims, the Customs Court and the Court of Customs and Patent Appeals. The Court of Claims hears contract claims against the government; the Customs Court deals with questions arising in the administration of the tariff laws; and the Court of Customs and Patent Appeals reviews decisions of the Customs Court and the Patent Office.

On the edge of the judicial system are the so-called "legislative" courts. These are courts established by Congress under some constitutional authority other than Article III. Examples are the former territorial courts of Alaska and Hawaii and the courts of such insular possessions as Guam and the Virgin Islands. These tribunals were created under Article IV, section 3, which gives Congress power to make all needful rules and regulations respecting the territory or other property belonging to the United States. The judge of a "legislative" court can be appointed for a term of years rather than "during good behavior," his salary is not guaranteed against reduction, and duties not strictly judicial can be required of him and his court. He might also be subject to removal by the President for cause.

The courts of the District of Columbia are created under Article I, section 8, clause 17, giving Congress the power "to exercise exclusive legislation" over the District. These courts have been held to be both "legislative" and "constitutional"; thus the tenure and pay of their judges are protected by Article III, but Congress can authorize them to exercise nonjudicial powers.

JURISDICTION

The jurisdiction of the Federal courts is defined by Article III on two different bases—subject matter and nature of the parties involved. The subject matter classifications are (1) all cases in law and equity arising under the Constitution; (2) all cases in law and equity arising under the laws of the United States; (3) all cases in law and equity arising under treaties made under the authority of the United States; and (4) all cases of admiralty and maritime jurisdiction. Any case falling in these four fields can be brought in the Federal courts, regardless of who the parties to the controversy may be.

Issues arising under the first three of these headings are referred to generally as "Federal questions." Such a case arises wherever an interpretation or application of the Constitution or a Federal statute or treaty is essential to a judicial decision. A plaintiff seeking to bring a case in the Federal courts on one of these grounds must set forth on the face of his complaint a substantial claim as to the Federal question involved. Cases appealed from state supreme courts are often refused review by the Supreme Court on the ground that no substantial Federal question is involved.

The second basis for Federal court jurisdiction is in terms of the parties involved. Article III extends Federal jurisdiction to controversies (1) to which the United States is a party; (2) between two or more states; (3) between a state and citizens of another state; (4) between citizens of different states; (5) between a state, or the citizens thereof, and foreign states, citizens, or subjects; and (6) to all cases affecting ambassadors, other public ministers, and consuls. Matters involving these classes of parties can be brought in the Federal courts, no matter what the subject matter.

Of these classes, the first and the fourth are by far the most important in the generation of litigation. The United States enters Federal courts as a party plaintiff in a great number of civil and criminal suits every year, and it can also be haled into court as a defendant in situations where it has waived its sovereign immunity and given its consent to be sued. When no consent to sue the government has been given, it may be possible to sue officials acting for the government, particularly if they are alleged to be acting beyond their statutory authority or under an unconstitutional statute.

Suits between citizens of different states are commonly referred to as "diversity of citizenship" cases. The purpose of opening the Federal courts to these cases was originally to provide a neutral forum for the determination of such disputes, since the state courts might be biased in favor of their own citizens and against "strangers" from other states. Today there is less likelihood of such bias, and many persons have urged the abolition of this class of Federal jurisdiction. In 1958 Congress undertook to reduce the number of such cases in the Federal courts by limiting them to disputes involving more than $10,000.

The provision extending Federal jurisdiction to suits between a state and citizens of another state was the source of a controversy which resulted in adoption of the Eleventh Amendment. In *Chisholm v. Georgia* (1793) the Supreme Court ruled that this language, which had been generally understood to be an authorization to each state to sue citizens of other states, also permitted citizens to sue a state other than their own. This judicial misreading of constitutional intent aroused a storm in the states, and Congress promptly responded by initiating the Eleventh Amendment to reverse this ruling.

Suits falling under Federal jurisdiction can also be brought in state courts, except in those areas—such as Federal criminal, admiralty, patent, and bankruptcy cases—where Congress has given the Federal courts exclusive jurisdiction. In all other areas the state and Federal courts enjoy concurrent jurisdiction over Article III cases. A suit meeting the tests of Federal jurisdiction which is filed in a state court can by appropriate action be transferred to a Federal court for trial. States have occasionally sought to place restrictions on the right of removal of civil suits from state to Federal courts, particularly where out-of-state corporations are concerned, but such laws have usually been declared unconstitutional.

Where state courts do exercise Federal jurisdiction, they are of course bound by the "supremacy clause" of the Constitution. Article VI, after making the Constitution, laws, and treaties of the United States "the supreme law of the land," continues: "And the judges in every state shall be bound thereby, anything in the Constitution or laws of any state to the contrary notwithstanding."

The complication of a dual system of courts is one which other leading Federal governments, such as Australia, Canada, and India, have avoided. In these countries there is only one Federal court, superimposed on a complete system of state courts. By contrast the American system may often seem to be cumbersome and productive of confusion and delays. However, processes of cooperation and adjustment have largely solved the many potential conflicts in our dual system of courts.

JUDICIAL POWER

The judicial power that the Constitution gives the Federal courts is the power to determine "cases" and "controversies" of the types specified in Article III. What is a case or controversy? Not every argument or dispute presented in the form of a lawsuit will qualify. To have a case or controversy in the constitutional sense there must be (1) adverse parties (2) who have a substantial legal interest (3) in a dispute arising out of facts, real, not hypothetical, (4) in which there can be an enforceable determination of the rights of the parties. These conditions are so well understood that they customarily raise no difficulties, but they do relieve the Court of passing on some broad public issues which cannot be fitted into the context of a traditional lawsuit.

The courts decide controversies by determining the facts in the dispute, and applying the law to those facts. According to the tradition of the English common law, on which American jurisprudence is largely based, the law is a body of general principles of right and justice embodied in the past decisions of the courts. The courts do not make law, it is said; they merely declare what it is in specific cases, applying established principles to new situations as they arise.

That this is, in part at least, a kind of lawmaking becomes obvious in a case in which the precedents are inconclusive, or conflicting, or in which there simply are no precedents. Often enough in such a case judges will lay down a rule based primarily on their own notions of public policy and the general interest and not on any specifically legal or juridical considerations.

The power of the Federal courts to enforce their decisions is normally taken for granted, but in fact the courts have no enforcement machinery at their direct disposal except for a few marshals. The judiciary must look to the President and to Congress for help in case of any real resistance to its orders. Andrew Jackson's purported comment, "John Marshall has made his decision, now let him enforce it," reveals the need of the Supreme Court for support by its governmental colleagues and the backing of public opinion.

THE FEDERAL JUDICIARY

The appointment of Federal judges is frankly and entirely a political process. With few exceptions the President limits his choice to members of his own party. From 1933 to 1962, for example, there were only two exceptions to this practice in Supreme Court appointments—President Truman's appointment of Republican Harold Burton, with whom he had been associated in the Senate, and President Eisenhower's naming of Democrat William Brennan, Jr. In the lower Federal courts, during the present century over 90 per cent of all judicial appointments have gone to members of the President's party.

District judgeships are filled primarily on the recommendation of the state party organization and the senator from the state, if there is one of the President's party. The nominees thus suggested are given a thorough check by the Department of Justice, the FBI, and the American Bar Association's committee on the Federal judiciary. Vacancies on the courts of appeals are sometimes filled by promotion of a district judge; the party organizations are still important in the choices at this level.

For the Supreme Court, the President receives suggestions from many sources, and particularly from his Attorney General, but he makes his own decision, and often he has his own ideas on the subject, either as to specific persons, or as to the qualifications he wants. Presidents usually concern themselves with the political viewpoint of a nominee, but predicting the future decisions of a potential appointee is of course risky business. The Senate confirmation stage also affords an opportunity for the political views of the nominee to be considered. Perhaps the most famous instance was the violent fight on Justice Brandeis when he was nominated by President Wilson in 1916. He was attacked by conservatives because of his alleged lack of "judicial temperament," but won confirmation on a straight party vote. Charles Evans Hughes was also unsuccessfully opposed in 1931, some liberal Democrats and agrarian Republicans picturing him as a "corporation lawyer." The nomination of John J. Parker was actually defeated in 1930 because of unjustified allegations that he was antilabor and anti-Negro.

Appointment of Federal judges for "good behavior" is one of the great pillars of judicial independence. A Federal judge can be removed from office only by conviction on impeachment. Only one Supreme Court justice has ever been subjected to impeachment proceedings, Samuel Chase, whose judicial conduct was marked by gross and violent Federalist partisanship. In 1804 the triumphant Jeffersonians sought reprisal by way of impeachment, but failed to secure a conviction. Only eight lower Federal court judges have been impeached in the entire history of the Federal bench, four of whom were convicted.

THE SUPREME COURT AND ITS OPERATION

The Supreme Court was originally composed of six judges, but the number was subsequently both reduced and increased by Congress.

usually with political motives in mind. Since 1869 the size has been stable at nine members, and the effort of President Roosevelt to increase the number of justices in 1937 failed. The Court is headed by the Chief Justice of the United States. His formal authority consists primarily in his role as presiding officer in court and at the conferences and in his power to assign the writing of opinions.

There are some special problems of jurisdiction relating to the Supreme Court. It is primarily an appellate court, but the Constitution does define two categories of cases which can be heard in the Court's original jurisdiction, i.e., without prior consideration by any other court. These are cases in which a state is a party, and those affecting ambassadors, public ministers, and consuls. However, the Court generally does not have to accept a suit invoking its original jurisdiction unless it feels that there is a compelling reason of public policy.

All the remaining business of the Supreme Court comes to it in its appellate jurisdiction, which it exercises, as the Constitution says, "with such exceptions, and under such regulations as the Congress shall make." In the post-Civil War period Congress used this authority over the Court's appellate jurisdiction to withdraw from its consideration a politically embarrassing case in which the Court had already heard argument. The Supreme Court agreed that such action was within congressional power. In 1957 Senator Jenner of Indiana sought reprisal against the Court's decisions in certain national security cases by a bill withdrawing the Court's appellate jurisdiction in five specific kinds of cases, but it failed of enactment.

Most of the cases the Supreme Court decides are brought before it by the writ of certiorari. This Latin word can be translated as "made more certain" or "better informed." It comes from the formal language of the old English writ of certiorari, by which a higher court ordered a lower court to send up the record of a case because the higher court wished to be better informed or more certain about the proceedings below.

Certiorari is a discretionary writ—that is, the Supreme Court does not have to grant a petition for certiorari and in most cases does not. Petitions are granted only in cases in which at least four of the nine judges agree that issues of special importance are presented.

Before a case can get to the Supreme Court it must have gone through the appropriate lower courts. The role of the Supreme Court is then to correct errors of law—that is, mistakes in defining, interpreting, or applying the law—made by the courts below. But not all judicial errors are important enough to require correction by the Supreme Court. In recent years the Supreme Court has granted less than 20 per cent of the petitions for certiorari filed annually. The exercise of the Court's discretion in deciding whether to grant or deny certiorari may involve as much judicial statesmanship as the decision of a case on the merits.

Congress has provided for review by appeal of state court decisions denying a litigant's claim of Federal right. A state court is said to have denied a claim of Federal right (1) where it upholds a state law which one of the parties contends violates the Federal Constitution, or (2) where one of the parties invokes a Federal statute or treaty and the state court holds it invalid. Decisions of these types can be appealed from the highest state court "in which a decision could be had."

The Supreme Court meets for business in October of every year, and this "October Term" continues until the following June. The usual pattern of the Court's operation is to hear the arguments of counsel in cases before it for about two weeks at a time and then to recess for two weeks or so to study the cases and write opinions.

On Fridays during the term, the justices meet in conferences to discuss and decide pending cases. At the conference the Chief Justice presents each case along with his views, and discussion then moves to the associate justices in order of seniority. When the vote is taken, the order is reversed, the most recent appointees to the Court voting first, and the Chief Justice last. Following the vote, the Chief Justice assigns the writing of the Court's opinion to himself or one of his colleagues. If the decision was not unanimous and the Chief Justice voted in the minority, the senior associate justice who voted in the majority controls the assignment of the decision. Drafts of opinions are circulated among the justices, and the author may revise the final opinion on the basis of comments by his colleagues.

In the Court's early days it was the custom for all justices to give their opinions seriatim in a case, and there was no single opinion "for the Court." However, when John Marshall became Chief Justice in 1801, he decided that the Court's prestige and power would be increased if a single opinion was prepared, and in fact he himself wrote the opinion in almost all important cases. Justices were still free to write concurring or dissenting opinions, but there was a tendency for them to go along with the Court in silence unless their disagreement was sharp. More recent practice permits dissents to be registered much more freely, and during many terms the non-unanimous decisions have outnumbered the unanimous ones.

It is a fundamental principle of American and English jurisprudence that a decision by the highest court in a jurisdiction is a binding precedent on the questions of law involved in the case. The court making the decision and all the courts subordinate to it are expected to follow the precedent and to give similar answers to similar questions whenever they arise thereafter. The Latin label for this rule is stare decisis, "to stand by the things decided."

Although stare decisis is an ancient and fundamental principle, the Supreme Court does not always follow it. Particularly in constitutional cases, the Court may find it necessary to disregard or overrule its own prior decisions. If the Court will not change its interpretation of the Constitution, it can be accomplished only by a formal amendment. Justice Brandeis[1] once wrote:

> Stare decisis is usually the wise policy, because in most matters it is more important that the applicable rule of law be settled than that it be settled right. . . . This is commonly true even where the error is a matter of serious concern, provided correction can be had by legislation. But in cases involving the Federal Constitution, where correction through legislative action is practically impossible, this Court has often overruled its earlier decisions. The Court bows to the lessons of experience and the force of better reasoning, recognizing that the process of trial and error, so fruitful in the physical sciences, is appropriate also in the judicial function.

JUDICIAL REVIEW

The most important responsibility of the Supreme Court is to interpret the Constitution of the United States. In carrying out that high duty the Court may find it necessary to nullify state statutes or even acts of Congress as violative of the Constitution.

The basic theory on which the American practice of judicial review is based may be summarized as follows. The written Constitution is a superior law, subject to change only by an extraordinary legislative

[1] *Burnet v. Coronado Oil & Gas Co.*, 205 U.S. 393 (1932).

process involving both Congress and the states, and as such superior to common and statutory law. The powers of the several departments of government are limited by the terms of the Constitution. The judges are expected to enforce the provisions of the Constitution as the higher law and to refuse to give effect to any legislative act or executive order in conflict therewith.

Now the curious thing is that there is nothing about this in the Constitution itself. The immediate source of the doctrine is the decision of Chief Justice John Marshall in the case of *Marbury v. Madison* (1803). The facts in this case were simple enough. Marbury had been appointed a justice of the peace for the District of Columbia by President Adams just before he went out of office in 1801. His commission was signed and sealed, but the Federalist Secretary of State, none other that John Marshall, failed to deliver it on March 3, and Jefferson on taking office instructed Madison not to deliver it. Marbury filed a petition for mandamus to compel Madison to deliver the commission. He filed it in the Supreme Court directly without any prior court proceedings, thus invoking the Court's original jurisdiction under the Judiciary Act of 1789.

A writ of mandamus (Latin for "we command") is an order to a court or a public official to perform some act required by law. The Supreme Court could grant Marbury's petition or deny it. At first glance, it seemed that the Court was bound to lose the contest for power and prestige whichever it did. If the writ was issued, Madison, with Jefferson's support, would refuse to obey it, and the Court would have no practical means of compelling him to do so. If the Court refused relief to Marbury, it would be admitting officially that it lacked any authority to control the executive. In either case, the judiciary and the Federalists would be humiliated and the triumph of Jefferson and the Democrats would be complete and obvious.

Marshall's decision was a masterful stroke. He ruled that the Judiciary Act of 1789, in authorizing the Supreme Court to grant writs of mandamus in its original jurisdiction, had unconstitutionally extended the Court's original jurisdiction beyond that provided for in the Constitution. The Court consequently declined to issue the writ, leaving Madison and Jefferson with nothing to defy or resist. But the writ was refused not because the Court lacked power to give relief against executive officers, but because the Court asserted and exercised the much greater power of passing on the constitutionality of an act of Congress.

Though the draftsmen of the Constitution had not specifically provided for this power, such evidence as there is of contemporary opinion and practice tends to support Marshall. Furthermore, though Marshall cited no precedent, state courts had already found occasion to strike down state statutes because they were in violation of state constitutions. Alexander Hamilton in No. 78 of *The Federalist* had argued strongly in favor of judicial review, an argument from which Marshall borrowed. And even the Democrats voiced no strong objections to the doctrine at the time, though they denounced Marshall's attempt to instruct Jefferson and Madison in the performance of their official duties. The Chief Justice's arguments may not have been unanswerable, but this conclusion that passing on the constitutionality of acts of Congress is one of the normal functions of the judiciary seems to have been pretty well accepted in 1803. It is, of course, firmly established today.

In more modern times, judicial review has been criticized as undemocratic, in that it turns basic policy decisions over to a lifetime judiciary responsible to no popular will. That there is room for judicial discretion in decisions on constitutionality cannot be doubted. Seldom is a statute so plainly and obviously in violation of the Constitution that there is not room for two opinions about it. Decisions on constitutional issues are likely to be as much a matter of social and economic philosophy as of logical deduction and immutable principles of law, and the fact that these decisions are made by nine men called judges sitting in a marble palace does not change the situation.

One method of countering the undemocratic charge is to admit it and then go on to point out that democratic nature or quality is not the sole test of an institution in the American system. The Constitution does not provide for a simple democratic regime, always directly responsive to majority will, but for a Federal representative republic equipped with a number of built-in checks and balances, of which judicial review is one.

Another answer also admits that the Supreme Court is undemocratic, but asserts that it is not dangerously so. The Court, it is said, is inherently so weak that it cannot long defy the settled determination of a substantial majority. When it has tried to do so, it has not been able to maintain its position long. Congress controls most of its jurisdiction, many of its powers, and even the number of its members. The execution of its judgments and the appointment of its members depend on the President. It is consequently by no means immune from popular and political pressures.

Within the present century, there have been two periods in which the Supreme Court's powers of review have become the subject of a major political struggle. One was occasioned by the Court's invalidation of many items in the New Deal's legislative program in 1935 and 1936. President Roosevelt retaliated in 1937 by requesting Congress to authorize six additional justices, increasing the Court's size to fifteen. This effort represented a serious political miscalculation on Mr. Roosevelt's part. While it was clear that the country disagreed with the Court's constitutional interpretations, it was equally opposed to any such rude laying of hands on the judicial institution. There are legitimate ways of changing judicial policy, but this was not one of them. Congress defeated the President's proposal, and instead passed a liberalized retirement act to encourage the older justices to leave the bench. Within a short time resignations permitted President Roosevelt to make over the Court by new appointments, and the judicial threat to executive and legislative policy was ended.

The Supreme Court of the 1950s also encountered a political storm as a result of its decisions on racial segregation in the public schools and certain national security cases in which it upheld the civil rights of Communists or persons accused of being Communists. This time it was Congress rather than the President which mounted an attack on the Supreme Court, but it failed just as completely as the "Court-packing" plan had failed. Again, however, the Court did withdraw from some of the positions which had led to congressional anger, particularly with respect to judicial control over congressional investigating committees.

The failure of both these efforts at Court curbing is full of significance for an understanding of the place of the Supreme Court in the American governmental system. The Court is at once a representative and a nonrepresentative institution, an instrument both of politics and justice. It is inevitable that Congress and the President will concern themselves with the Court's decisions, but this interest must be expressed in a way which will not damage the essential values of the judicial institution.

JUDICIAL SELF-RESTRAINT

The Supreme Court recognizes, in principle, that its power to construe the Constitution, and particularly its power to declare acts of Congress unconstitutional, must be exercised with great restraint. Consequently it approaches constitutional questions with reluctance, and will normally decide cases on a constitutional issue only when there seem to be no feasible alternatives.

The easiest means of avoiding constitutional questions is, of course, to deny certiorari in cases where such an issue is present, and this the Court sometimes does. Again, in a case which the Court has agreed to hear, decision may be delayed until the heat has gone out of a constitutional question. Several wartime civil liberties cases have not been decided until after the war was over.

The Supreme Court has, furthermore, imposed upon itself a comprehensive body of rules aimed at encouraging judicial self-restraint and avoiding constitutional decisions. As summarized by Justice Brandeis in his concurring opinion in *Ashwander v. Tennessee Valley Authority* (1936), these include the following: (1) The Court will not anticipate a question of constitutionality in advance of the necessity of deciding it, nor is it the habit of the Court to decide questions of a constitutional nature unless absolutely necessary to a decision of the case in hand. (2) The Court will not formulate a rule of constitutional law broader than is required by the precise facts to which it is to be applied. (3) The Court will not pass upon a constitutional question, although properly presented by the record, if there is also present some other ground upon which the case may be disposed of. (4) When the validity of an act of Congress is drawn into question, and even if a serious doubt of constitutionality is raised, it is a cardinal principle that the Court will first ascertain whether a construction of the statute is fairly possible by which the question may be avoided.

Whether or not the Court always follows these rules, they do reflect the general principles of its approach to judicial review. Beyond these maxims of judicial self-restraint, there are certain more technical rules applied to limit the breadth and freedom of the Supreme Court's approach to constitutional issues.

One of these is the rule that the question must be "justiciable." This means that judicial proceedings must meet the tests of cases and controversies already mentioned. The Court will not give "advisory opinions," even if requested by the President, as Washington once did. It is usually quick to detect and to refuse to rule on made-up cases which are in reality nothing but attempts to obtain a Supreme Court ruling on abstract questions of law, or "friendly" lawsuits where the parties on both sides have the same interests.

In 1895, for example, the Federal income tax was declared unconstitutional in a suit brought by a corporate stockholder against the corporation to prevent it from paying the tax. It seems unlikely that the corporation fought very hard to uphold its obligation to pay the tax. This particular decision was, in effect, overruled by the adoption of the Sixteenth Amendment, but the problem of representation of the public interest in constitutional litigation was not dealt with until 1937, when Congress provided that the United States must be joined as a party in any case in which the constitutionality of a Federal statute was questioned.

An important element of justiciability is "standing to sue." Not everyone with enough money to bring a lawsuit is entitled to litigate the legality or constitutionality of government action in the Federal courts. To have the standing necessary to maintain such an action, the plaintiff must establish the sufficiency of his interest in the controversy, and this means satisfying the courts on two main issues: (1) that his interest is one that is peculiar and personal to him and not one he shares with all other citizens generally, and (2) that the interest he is defending is a legally recognized and protected right immediately threatened by some government action.

Controversies which meet the test of justiciability are nevertheless occasionally refused adjudication by the Supreme Court on the ground that they involve "political questions." Where the authority to make a certain decision appears to have been assigned by the Constitution exclusively to the Congress or the President, the courts will refuse to interfere, although the case may be otherwise justiciable. The conclusion that the Constitution assigns authority to solve a particular problem to the two political branches of the government is usually supported by practical considerations.

Thus it is generally agreed that the Constitution gives the President almost exclusive authority over American relations with foreign governments. It follows, and the courts agree, that a question related to the conduct of foreign affairs is likely to be a political question with which the judiciary should not meddle. Again, the whole process of amending the Constitution is now regarded by the Supreme Court as a political question within the jurisdiction of Congress. Whether a state has a "republican form of government," such as the Constitution guarantees to every state in Article IV, section 4, is another political question.

The Supreme Court has not been too sure whether the apportionment of seats in the House of Representatives and state legislatures is a political question. In *Colegrove v. Green* (1946), a badly divided Court refused to remedy gross inequalities of population in Illinois congressional districts, where one congressman might represent nine times as many people as a representative from another Illinois district. The Court majority thought it should keep out of this "political thicket." Similarly the Court in 1950 refused to look at the Georgia county unit system for voting in primary elections, though it intentionally discriminates against the large city populations in favor of the rural areas.

In 1962, however, the Supreme Court reversed this position in *Baker v. Carr*, holding that the Federal courts could review a claim of malapportionment of seats in the Tennessee state legislature. The Tennessee constitution required reapportionment of the legislature every 10 years, but no action had been taken since 1901, and consequently the districts varied greatly in population. The *Baker v. Carr* ruling raises many difficult questions about the future role of the judiciary in handling these partisan apportionment issues, but since unrepresentative legislators are not likely to vote themselves out of office, some possibility of appeal to the courts seems required.

SUMMARY

American courts participate to a significant and unusual degree in the policy-forming process. Selection of Federal judges is political in that they are generally selected by the President from members of his own party and have typically been active politically. However, the standards for selection are strict, and the Federal bench is of high prestige and unquestioned integrity. Because of their life tenure and independence, the Federal judiciary can act as a check on both the President and Congress. The Supreme Court is recognized as the highest authority on the meaning of the Constitution, and it can nullify statutes or executive actions as unconstitutional. The exercise of this power has occasionally led to serious counterattacks on the Court, but in general the Court has acted with a sense of restraint, and has kept out of certain types of "political" questions, so that it has weathered all storms and safeguarded its status as keeper of the Constitution.

Review Questions

1. What are the three levels of the Federal judicial system?

2. Why can "diversity of citizenship" cases be tried in Federal courts?

3. What are the elements in a judicial "case or controversy"?

4. How are Federal judges chosen?

5. How do cases get to the Supreme Court?

6. What is the procedure by which the Supreme Court decides cases?

7. What is the responsibility of the Supreme Court to follow its precedents?

8. What was the dilemma Marshall faced in *Marbury v. Madison,* and how did he solve it?

9. Is judicial review undemocratic?

10. What principles of judicial self-restraint has the Supreme Court announced?

INDIVIDUAL RIGHTS

Chapter 6

The American tradition of civil rights is composed of many strands. Basic is the Christian-Hebraic belief in the worth of the individual, and acceptance of a moral obligation to shape the institutions of society so that they will promote the unfolding and the enrichment of human character. Centuries of struggle in England to achieve political practices which would aim toward equality before the law and equalization of political power were a living part of the early American tradition. The writings of the seventeenth- and eighteenth-century political philosophers, particularly Locke, with their stress on natural law and the origins of government in a compact freely entered into by its citizens, were an essential element in American revolutionary thought.

All this was the heritage of the new nation, the "common law" of American liberties. If these ideals had never been spelled out in the Constitution, they would no doubt have continued to be effective. But placing them in the Bill of Rights provided a guide for the political decisions of the developing commonwealth, and made these principles judicially enforceable.

THE RIGHT TO VOTE

In a very real sense, the right to vote is the foundation on which all other rights are based. The disfranchised can appeal to the sense of justice of the franchise holders, and they can endeavor to protect their rights in the courts, but they can never be full-fledged members of the political community. Without the sanctions of political pressure exercised through the ballot box, their liberties will inevitably be more limited and less secure than those of the voting members of the community. The experience of Negroes in the South over the past century is ample illustration.

The drafters of the Constitution dealt with the franchise problem in a rather indirect manner. They provided in Article I, section 2, that persons eligible to vote for members of the House in the several states "shall have the qualifications requisite for electors of the most numerous branch of the state legislature." By this method the Constitution[1] assured election of the House of Representatives on a popular base but avoided creation of a national electorate different from the state electorates, which were defined by legal provisions varying widely from state to state.

Under this arrangement the states determine which of their citizens have the privilege of the franchise. However, once a state has decided by statutory provisions who is eligible to vote, then the Constitution through Article I, section 2, steps in to guarantee their *right* to vote in Federal elections.

In addition, three amendments have a bearing on elections and the electorate. The equal protection clause of the Fourteenth Amendment has been applied to forbid discriminatory practices by state election officials. The Fifteenth Amendment specifically guarantees that "the right of citizens of the United States to vote shall not be denied or abridged by the United States or by any state on account of race,

---

[1] The drafters of the Constitution had to deal with the franchise problem only in connection with the election of members of the House, since senators were chosen by the state legislatures, and presidential electors were appointed in such manner as the state legislatures might direct.

color, or previous condition of servitude." The Nineteenth Amendment, adopted in 1920, uses the same formula to guarantee women the right to vote.

Application of constitutional protections to primary elections was for some time in serious question. In 1921 the Supreme Court held that when the Constitution referred to elections, it meant the "final choice of an officer by the duly qualified electors," and that the primary was "in no real sense part of the manner of holding the election." Applying this principle in 1935, the Court ruled that there was no constitutional barrier to exclusion of Negroes from the Democratic primaries in Texas, provided the discrimination was not state-authorized and was achieved solely by the action of the political party conducting the primary.

These two notions, that primaries are not part of the election process, and that political parties are in effect "private clubs" which can exclude any persons they do not like from their primaries, were both obviously fallacious, and both were soon abandoned by the Court. The Constitution was held applicable to primaries in *United States v. Classic* (1941), a prosecution brought by the Federal government against election officials in Louisiana who had tampered with the ballots in a primary where candidates for representatives in Congress were chosen. The Court pointed out that the Louisiana election laws made the primary "an integral part" of the process of electing congressmen, and that in fact the Democratic primary in Louisiana was "the only stage of the election procedure" where the voters' choice was of significance.

The private club theory was abandoned in *Smith v. Allwright* (1944). The Court held that after the *Classic* ruling, party primaries could no longer be regarded as private affairs nor the parties conducting them as unaffected with public responsibilities. Noting that parties and party primaries in Texas were in fact regulated at many points by state statutes, the Court reasoned that a party required to follow these directions was "an agency of the State," and if it practiced discrimination against Negroes, that was "state action within the meaning of the Fifteenth Amendment."

Supreme Court decisions alone, however, were not enough to break the widespread practice of Negro exclusion from the polls. In 1957 Congress passed a new Civil Rights Act, the first since Reconstruction days. The act authorized Federal prosecuting officers to secure injunctions against actual or threatened interference with the right to vote in the states, whereas it had previously been necessary for the individual voter to take the initiative in bringing suit to protect his rights of suffrage.

The statute also created a Civil Rights Commission to take testimony, gather information on denial of voting and other constitutionally protected rights, and make recommendations to Congress on needed legislation. Hearings held by this Commission spotlighted the barriers against Negro registration and voting in several Southern states. However, by 1960 only four suits had been brought by the Department of Justice under the act.

In that year Congress passed another Civil Rights Act intended to assist Negroes in securing registration. Referees appointed by Federal judges were empowered to register for voting, in Federal and state elections, qualified Negroes who had been refused registration in areas where a pattern of discrimination had been established by suits under the 1957 statute. The act also made voting records public, required their preservation, and gave the Attorney General access to them—steps intended to facilitate Federal protection of voting rights.

The 1960 measure was a compromise which was not expected to prove very effective. In 1961 the Commission on Civil Rights reported that discriminatory disfranchisement still existed in about 100 counties in eight Southern states. In at least 13 counties where Negroes were a majority of the population, not one was registered to vote. Since these results are often achieved by poll tax requirements and the discriminatory administration of literacy tests for voting, recent proposals for congressional legislation have centered on these areas. In 1962 Congress passed and sent to the states for ratification a constitutional amendment barring the requirement of a poll tax as a qualification for voting in Federal elections.

FREEDOM OF SPEECH AND PRESS

The First Amendment is the basic constitutional charter of American civil liberties. It provides: "Congress shall make no law . . . abridging the freedom of speech, or of the press." On its face this is a clear and absolute barrier to any congressional abridgment of these freedoms. But we are all familiar with situations where speech is abridged or restrained, with common consent. One may not talk freely in a library reading room, or during a church service, or while a court is in session. There are rules of order governing legislative assemblies or public meetings, which restrain two people from talking at the same time, or which prevent speech irrelevant to the issue under discussion. One who talks another person into committing a crime is a guilty partner in that crime.

The "freedom of speech" is obviously not involved in such restrictions. This concept relates rather to the right of discussion of public issues, free from governmental restraint, in the press or in the normal channels of public contact. But even here there are times and circumstances when the government thinks it necessary to clamp down restraints on discussion or printing. During World War I, for example, Congress passed the Espionage and Sedition Acts under which a substantial number of persons were jailed for criticizing the war effort or hampering it in some way. The Supreme Court had to decide whether such punishment for speech offenses was permissible under the First Amendment.

The argument, of course, was that when words are used to accomplish illegal acts, such as inciting to violence or hindering recruiting, the words themselves become tainted with the illegality of the acts and can be punished. The problem is, how closely must the speech be related to the crime in order for the speech itself to become punishable? How clear must the purpose be to incite to crime?

Justice Oliver Wendell Holmes was the spokesman for the Court in its first encounters with these World War I cases, and he developed the famous "clear and present danger" test to measure the extent of the Federal government's powers to punish the spoken or written word because of its connection with illegal action. He wrote:

> The question in every case is whether the words used are used in such circumstances and are of such a nature as to create a clear and present danger that they will bring about the substantive evils that Congress has a right to prevent. It is a question of proximity and degree.

During wartime, he added, many things that might be said in time of peace cannot be "endured."

Thus he argued in *Schenck v. United States* (1919) that persons mailing circulars to men urging them not to register for the draft could be punished. But he soon found other situations where he and Justice Brandeis disagreed with the rest of the Court on whether "clear and present danger" had been shown to exist. It became obvious that this test could give differing results, depending upon who was applying it, and in fact it kept no one out of jail during the post-World War I hysteria.

The First Amendment refers specifically to Congress, but in 1925 the Supreme Court took an extremely important step in expanding the constitutional protection of speech and press to cover action by the states as well. The Court held in *Gitlow v. New York* (1925) that the "liberty" which the Fourteenth Amendment protects against infringement by the states without due process includes the freedoms mentioned in the First Amendment. Thus the principles of the First Amendment achieved universal applicability in American government.

CENSORSHIP

There are in general two ways in which governments may deny freedom of speech or press. The first is by censorship, that is, imposing in advance legal limits which prohibit or otherwise effectively restrain speaking or publishing. The second is by punishing persons because what they have actually said or printed is alleged to violate the law.

Censorship, or prior restraint, is generally regarded as more dangerous to freedom of expression than subsequent punishment, and the American tradition has been strongly against censorship. The Supreme Court has on several important occasions acted to protect newspapers or even handbills from official suppression. However, it is not censorship to apply normal business regulatory statutes such as the Sherman Antitrust Act or the National Labor Relations Act against newspaper publishers.

The holding of public meetings or speaking in public places is also generally safeguarded against censorship. In *Kunz v. New York* (1951) the Supreme Court denied the right of New York City to remove a bigoted preacher from the public streets by use of a permit requirement for street preaching. But police permission may be required for public street meetings which create a traffic problem. Again, the Court has held that loud and raucous sound trucks may be forbidden by a municipality.

Picketing as a method of giving public information concerning the facts of a labor dispute was placed by the Supreme Court under the protection of the free speech clause in 1940. However, the Court subsequently held that the potentialities of violence and coercion which attend picketing give state legislatures and courts control authority which they would not have over more normal types of expression.

State censorship of motion pictures was approved by the Supreme

Court in 1915. Later, however, the movies came to have some standing in the world of ideas, and in *Burstyn v. Wilson* (1952), the Supreme Court overruled the 1915 decision and struck down the New
York movie censorship law on the ground that the standards it fixed
were much too broad. In a number of subsequent cases the Court
voided other state censorship laws or actions taken under them, but
refused to say that all censorship of motion pictures is necessarily
unconstitutional.

SUBSEQUENT PUNISHMENT

Punishment for speech offenses is probably attempted most often on
grounds that the speaker had threatened the maintenance of public
order. Clearly, preservation of the peace is a prime responsibility of
a community's officials. In all states there are statutes punishing breach
of the peace, disorderly conduct, inciting to riot, and the like, in which
speech may be involved.

In the application of such statutes against alleged speech offenses the
judicial problem is always one of balancing the gravity of the offense
against the seriousness of the limits imposed on the circulation of ideas.
Thus in *Chaplinsky v. New Hampshire* (1942) a member of Jehovah's
Witnesses who had called a city marshal a "damned Fascist" was convicted of violating a state statute against calling anyone "offensive or
derisive" names in public. The Court upheld the conviction, saying that
insults "are no essential part of any exposition of ideas, and are of such
slight value as a step to truth that any benefit that may be derived
from them is clearly outweighed by the social interest in order and
morality."

Again, freedom of speech does not justify libel or slander, and
persons responsible for statements of such a character can be prosecuted. A libel is any written or printed statement defaming or reflect-
ing on the character of a person, published maliciously and without
justification. A slander is an oral statement of the same kind.

Obscenity, like libel, has long been punishable under state laws, and
there is also a Federal obscenity statute applying to the mails. Punishment of obscenity has generally been regarded as raising no constitutional question. In *Roth v. United States* (1957) the Supreme Court
held that obscenity is "not within the area of constitutionally protected speech." The First Amendment extends to "all ideas having even
the slightest redeeming social importance—unorthodox ideas, controversial ideas, even ideas hateful to the prevailing climate of opinion."
But obscenity is "utterly without redeeming social importance."

However, courts have found it very difficult to determine whether particular publications are obscene, or to agree on the tests for obscenity. Views on this subject have become substantially more lenient in recent decades. In the *Roth* case the Court's opinion defined the test as "whether to the average person, applying contemporary community standards, the dominant theme of the material taken as a whole appeals to prurient interest."

FREEDOM OF ASSOCIATION

There is no provision in the Constitution specifically protecting freedom of association, yet the right of individuals to organize into groups for political, economic, religious, and social purposes is universally recognized. The constitutional basis for this freedom derives from the right of assembly and the freedoms of speech, press, and religion. Of course associational freedom is not absolute for any group, but the liberal state seeks to encourage the maximum of group freedom compatible with the general welfare. Restrictions on associational freedom must meet stringent constitutional tests.

The recent experiences of two organizations can best illustrate the issues in this field. The Communist Party and other communist-oriented organizations and their members have been subjected to a wide variety of restrictions and punishments. The Federal government has acted principally under the Smith Act of 1940, which punishes advocating or teaching the violent overthrow of any government in the United States, or organizing or knowingly becoming a member of a group which so advocates.

The Supreme Court affirmed the constitutionality of this act in *Dennis v. United States* (1951), a case in which 11 leaders of the American Communist Party were convicted for organizing and leading the party. The Court held that, so far as the communist threat was concerned, the clear and present danger test "cannot mean that before the Government may act, it must wait until the *putsch* is about to be executed, the plans have been laid and the signal is awaited." Ten years later, in a case involving an active Communist leader the Court also upheld the Smith Act provision making "knowing" membership in an organization advocating the forcible overthrow of the government a crime.

Another statutory weapon against the Communist Party was the Subversive Activities Control Act of 1950. This act ordered communist-action organizations to register with the Attorney General, and a special board was set up to determine which organizations should be required to register. Following issuance of such an order, the organization must supply to the government complete information on its officers and finances, any mail or radio broadcasts it sends out must be identified as communist propaganda, its members commit a crime if they apply for or use a United States passport, and there are various other consequences. The Supreme Court upheld the constitutionality of the registration requirement as applied to the Communist Party in 1961, but refused to pass on the validity of any of the various sanctions against members of the party until they were actually applied.

The Communist Party has thus been denied the usual constitutional rights of organizations, since the Supreme Court has concluded that Congress could justifiably regard the party as a threat to the national security because of its goals and methods and its subservience to a foreign power. However, a strong minority on the Supreme Court has dissented in all these decisions, on the ground that the Communist Party members were being punished for what they advocated or taught, not because of any subversive or destructive acts.

The National Association for the Advancement of Colored People has also been under severe attack in recent years, but unlike the case of the Communist Party, the Supreme Court has protected its associational rights as a lawful organization with nonviolent goals. The pressure on the NAACP has come from Southern states which resent the activities of this organization in promoting desegregation in the public schools. For example, Alabama ordered the NAACP to register as an out-of-state corporation and, among other records, to give the names and addresses of its members in the state. The organization produced all the information required except the names and addresses, refusing to provide them on the ground that the members would be subject to social and economic pressure or even to physical attacks. The Supreme Court unanimously ruled against Alabama, concluding that compelled disclosure of the membership lists could interfere with the rights of individuals to engage in lawful association in support of their common beliefs.

FREEDOM OF RELIGION

Freedom to worship God according to the dictates of individual conscience was one of the dominant motives in the founding of the American Colonies, and it might have been expected that provisions guaranteeing that right would have an important place in the Constitution.

In fact, the founders left the original document almost devoid of language on the relationships of government and religion. The sole exception was the provision of Article VI that "no religious test shall ever be required as a qualification to any office or public trust under the United States."

The adoption of the First Amendment repaired the omissions of the original Constitution. The language of the amendment was specifically limited to Congress, though many states had similar provisions in their own constitutions. In 1940, however, the Supreme Court held that the freedom of religion clause in the First Amendment had been extended to the states by the Fourteenth Amendment's guarantee of "liberty."

The same principles that prevent prior restraint of speech or press also apply to religious observances or practices. It is unconstitutional for a state to require religious or philanthropic groups to get the consent of a public official before soliciting for funds. Again, the Supreme Court has held that Jehovah's Witnesses, who sell their literature from door to door, cannot be required to pay the license taxes imposed on other peddlers, since this would be a restraint on a religious observance.

Oregon raised a fundamental issue of religious liberty in 1922 when the state adopted a compulsory education act requiring all children to attend public schools for the first eight grades. This law would have deprived parents of the option of sending their children to religious or other nonpublic schools. In *Pierce v. Society of Sisters* (1925) the Supreme Court unanimously held the law invalid. The Court has also ruled that public schools may not compel students to participate in the exercise of saluting the flag if they have religious objections to such a ceremony.

Of course, claims of religious freedom cannot be used to justify violation of the criminal laws of the land. Thought and belief are protected, but actions or practices which are made criminal by law or are outrageously offensive to public morals are not rendered immune from punishment because of alleged religious motivation. Thus polygamy as practiced by members of the early Mormon Church was punished with the approval of the Supreme Court.

ESTABLISHMENT OF RELIGION

When the First Amendment forbade Congress to pass any law "respecting an establishment of religion," it outlawed any system of an established church such as still exists in England, where there is one official church entitled to public financial support. However, the essential features of this system had largely been eliminated in America by the time the First Amendment was adopted. There were various other forms of assistance to religion out of public funds, however, which the establishment provision was presumably intended to terminate.

Establishment issues have been raised periodically in American history over such matters as the official designation of Thanksgiving Day, the provision of chaplains for Congress and in the armed services, or compulsory chapel services at West Point and Annapolis. However, there was comparatively little discussion of the establishment clause by the Supreme Court until the issue was raised in a 1947 case from New Jersey. Under authorization by the state, a New Jersey township had reimbursed parents of public and Catholic school pupils for the transportation of their children to school on regular public transportation. The Supreme Court agreed that the establishment clause applied to the states because of the Fourteenth Amendment, but by a 5 to 4 vote went on to uphold the payments to parents of parochial school students.

Justice Black, writing the majority opinion, attempted to formulate a statement of what the establishment clause had come to mean:

> Neither a state nor the Federal Government can set up a church. Neither can pass laws which aid one religion, aid all religions, or prefer one religion over another. Neither can force nor influence a person to go to or to remain away from church against his will or force him to profess a belief or disbelief in any religion. No person can be punished for entertaining or professing religious beliefs or disbeliefs, for church attendance or non-attendance. No tax in any amount, large or small, can be levied to support any religious activities or institutions, whatever they may be called, or whatever form they may adopt to teach or practice religion.

On the basis of these principles Justice Black acknowledged that the New Jersey statute approached the verge of constitutional power. However, he was able to uphold transportation payment by regarding the law as "welfare legislation" the benefits of which should not be denied to any individuals "because of their faith, or lack of it. . . ." But Justice Rutledge, one of the dissenters, thought that transportation "is as essential to education as any other element," and added that if providing transportation to religious schools is merely "public welfare legislation," then there can be "no possible objection to more extensive support of religious education by New Jersey."

Religious exercises or training in the public schools have seemed to the Supreme Court to be clearly contrary to the establishment clause. The New York Board of Regents composed a short "non-denominational" prayer which they recommended be said aloud by each public school class at the beginning of every school day. The schools which adopted this procedure did not require students to participate; those who preferred could stand mute or leave the room.

In *Engel v. Vitale* (1962) the Supreme Court with only one dissent held that this was clearly a "religious activity." Justice Black said: "the constitutional prohibition against laws respecting an establishment of religion must at least mean that in this country it is no part of the business of government to compose official prayers for any group of the American people to recite as a part of a religious program carried on by government."

Another establishment problem was raised for the Court by the various "released time" programs for providing religious education in connection with the public schools. In 1948 the Court passed on such a program in the schools of Champaign, Illinois, under which public school children, on consent of their parents, attended classes in Protestant, Catholic, or Jewish religious instruction during school hours and in the school buildings. The religious teachers were not paid by the schools, but were under the supervision of the school superintendents, and attendance was compulsory for participants in the program. The Court, with only one dissent, held this arrangement unconstitutional since tax-supported school buildings were being used in propagating religious doctrines, and the public school machinery was being employed to provide pupils for religious classes.

This decision was widely attacked in church circles, and the criticism apparently had some effect. Four years later the Court modified its stand and approved a New York City released time program which differed from the Champaign plan in that the instruction took place off the school premises.

Public aid to religious schools has been a key problem in congressional discussions of Federal aid to education. In 1961 President Kennedy's educational bill failed of enactment because of this problem. The administration took the position that general across-the-board grants or loans to religious schools would be clearly unconstitutional, but suggested that it might be permissible to lend funds to church schools for special purposes not closely related to religious instruction, such as science or language training.

In 1961 the Court decided that state laws requiring the closing of commercial establishments on Sunday did not amount to an establishment of religion. The Court admitted that the Sunday closing laws had a religious origin, but maintained that they had now become secular regulations aiming to provide a uniform day of rest for all citizens. Two of these cases were brought by Orthodox Jews who observe Saturday as the Sabbath, but the Court did not believe that a law requiring them to close their shops on Sunday was an interference with their religious freedom.

PROCEDURES IN
CRIMINAL PROSECUTIONS

One of the basic concerns of the American Constitution is that persons shall not be deprived of life, liberty, or property without due process of law, which means a fair trial with all the procedural protections which have been developed in the Anglo-Saxon legal system. Half of the Bill of Rights—the Fourth through the Eighth Amendments—is devoted to stating the constitutional standards controlling criminal prosecutions, which indicates the importance these matters had in the eyes of the framers.

The Fourth Amendment protects the people in their "persons, houses, papers, and effects" from "unreasonable" searches and seizures. This provision gives effect to the ancient English maxim that a man's home is his castle. As the test of reasonableness, the Amendment relied primarily upon requirement of a search warrant, issued "upon probable cause, supported by oath or affirmation, and particularly describing the place to be searched, and the persons or things to be seized." Warrants must be obtained from judicial officers, who are expected to prevent overzealous or unjustified police action. Searches and seizures may be made without search warrants in connection with lawful arrests, but evidence of crime which is seized without warrant and without justification by the police cannot be used as evidence in a judicial prosecution.

Wire tapping was held by the Supreme Court in 1928 not to constitute illegal search and seizure, though Justice Holmes, dissenting, condemned it as a "dirty business." However, Congress has by statute made evidence secured by wire tapping inadmissible in the Federal courts.

An important provision in the Fifth Amendment is that no one "shall be compelled in any criminal case to be a witness against himself." This protection has been interpreted to cover witnesses before congressional committees and grand juries as well as defendants in criminal cases. There has been sharp difference of opinion about the virtue of the self-incrimination provision. However, this protection embodies a basic principle of Anglo-Saxon jurisprudence that no individual is obliged to help the government prove that he has been guilty of a crime.

The Constitution requires indictment by grand jury for capital or "otherwise infamous" crimes. This is a restraint on prosecuting officials, who must convince a citizen jury that there is substantial evidence of crime before a prosecution can be brought.

The defendant in a criminal case is guaranteed a jury trial by the Sixth Amendment. He must be informed of the nature and cause of the accusation, confronted with the witnesses against him, and have the assistance of legal counsel for his defense. In addition to these more specific guarantees, the Supreme Court accepts a general obligation to ensure the "fairness" of all criminal proceedings in the Federal courts.

The Supreme Court ruled as early as 1833 that the protections of the Bill of Rights applied only against the national government, not the states. However, the Fourteenth Amendment adopted due process as a standard binding on the states, thus opening the way for Supreme Court review of state judicial proceedings. The Court's basic problem has been to determine whether the states should be required to observe the same court procedures that the Bill of Rights imposes in Federal cases. The policy it has worked out has been a rather complicated one, involving a distinction between protections which are basic to a free society, and others which, while important, are not absolutely essential in a system of "ordered liberty."

Thus the Court has held that notice and hearing are fundamental attributes of a judicial system, and also that unreasonable searches and seizures are forbidden to the states. On the other hand, the states are not required to indict by grand jury, they can depart from the common law trial jury of 12, and they are not bound by the Federal rule on immunity from self-incrimination. For the states to adopt their own practices on these matters would not, the Court has said, violate a "principle of justice so rooted in the traditions and conscience of our people as to be ranked as fundamental."

A persistent minority on the Court has questioned the constitutionality of this double standard for Federal and state prosecutions, with some recent success in at least one field. In *Wolf v. Colorado* (1949) the Court ruled that, even though unreasonable searches and seizures by the states were unconstitutional, the evidence thus secured could nevertheless be used in state courts to secure a conviction for crime. This holding was directly contrary to the rule in the Federal courts, and it was subjected to continuing attack, until finally in *Mapp v. Ohio* (1961) the Court reversed the *Wolf* doctrine and applied the Federal rule to the states also.

EQUAL PROTECTION OF THE LAWS

Equal protection of the laws is an obligation imposed on the states by the Fourteenth Amendment, but in fact it is inherent in the concept of due process and so is binding on the Federal government also. The principle of equal protection does not mean that all class legislation or legal discrimination is invalid. Men can be treated differently from women; aliens have different obligations from citizens; large employers can be regulated differently from small employers; property in one section of a city can be zoned for uses forbidden in other sections of the city. But what equal protection does demand is that all persons in the same situation have the same privileges and be subject to the same legal obligations.

The equal protection clause has had a long history of use in testing economic and commercial regulations, but its greatest significance has been to protect against racial discrimination. The Fourteenth Amendment was adopted primarily to safeguard the rights of the newly freed Negroes after the Civil War, though of course it did not attain, nor has it yet attained, that goal. Racial discrimination is not something that can be abolished by constitutional provision or judicial fiat. But the equal protection standard has been the foundation for increasingly important judicial pressure toward that goal.

As early as 1886 the Supreme Court struck down a San Francisco ordinance which, under the guise of a safety regulation, was actually aimed at Chinese laundries. In 1935 the Court took note of the fact that no Negro had ever been called for jury duty in a particular Alabama county and gave notice that it would void criminal convictions of Negroes obtained under those conditions. In 1948 the Court held that state courts would violate the Fourteenth Amendment if they enforced restrictive covenants under which landowners agree among themselves not to sell their property to Negroes or other minority racial groups.

By all odds the most significant judicial blow against racial discrimination was *Brown v. Board of Education* (1954), in which the Supreme Court held racial segregation in the public schools unconstitutional. The Court itself had created the principal legal argument in support of segregation in 1896, when it had ruled that segregating the races in interstate transportation was valid if equal accommodations were offered to both races. This doctrine of "separate but equal" was finally overruled in the *Brown* decision, the Court holding that segregated educational facilities, even though equal in their physical aspects, were "inherently unequal" and deprived the children of the minority group of equal educational opportunities.

Naturally the Court was concerned about the problem of enforcing a ruling which demanded the abolition of passionately held social practices in whole sections of the country. After an additional hearing, the Court sent the cases which had been decided in *Brown* back to the Federal district courts in which they had originated, and instructed the district judges to require local school boards to proceed with plans for desegregation "with all deliberate speed."

At first it seemed that the prestige of the Court might substantially temper the expected resistance to the decree. The Supreme Court may have expected that it would receive some support from Congress and the President in winning acceptance for its ruling, but no such aid was forthcoming. On the contrary, 96 Southern congressmen signed a manifesto in 1956 challenging the legality of the Court's decision, and President Eisenhower, while declaring that he would enforce the law, persistently declined to attempt any organization of popular support for the desegregation ruling. Thus the responsibility for effecting this tremendous social revolution was left to some 58 Federal district and court of appeals judges in the Southern states, many of whom were personally opposed to the principle of the *Brown* decision.

Under these circumstances it was not surprising that progress toward the goal of desegregation was slow and uneven. In the border states a considerable measure of integration was achieved, but in the "old South" almost complete frustration of desegregation efforts was achieved by a variety of methods. The most publicized resistance was that organized by legislation in Virginia, and the violence associated with integration of the Little Rock high school in Arkansas.

The Supreme Court apparently chose deliberately not to intervene in the judicial controversies of the first few years, but in 1958 when a district judge ordered a 2½-year delay in the modest Little Rock integration program, the Supreme Court met in an unusual special summer session and upheld the court of appeals reversal of this order. The Supreme Court flatly charged that the governor and legislature of Arkansas had caused the violent resistance in that state, and reaffirmed the constitutional obligations of the states to obey the Court's mandate.

Continued progress toward integration depends upon a number of factors. First, local pressure by organized Negro groups, nearly always the National Association for the Advancement of Colored People, is usually necessary in order to get the issue raised in a local school system. In some sections of the South the reprisals against those active in the NAACP are so severe and so effective that there is simply no one who will speak up about segregated schools.

Second, there are the local school boards which, acting on their own initiative or under the compulsion of a district court order, must prepare a desegregation plan. School boards, even when they are willing to act, have usually preferred to act under the pressure of a court order in order to justify themselves to the segregationists in the community.

Third, there are the state legislatures which, usually under the governor's leadership, have in all Southern states passed a bewildering variety of laws aimed to prevent or to punish steps toward integration. These laws are generally known even by their sponsors to be unconstitutional, but the process of litigation takes time and delays any steps toward desegregation. The only one of these types of laws which has received any support from the Supreme Court was the Alabama pupil placement law, authorizing education authorities to place pupils in schools on the basis of various criteria, among which race is not mentioned. While there is no doubt that such statutes are intended to defeat integration, the Supreme Court's position was that the Alabama law was not unconstitutional on its face, and that consequently it could not be voided until evidence was presented of its use for illegal purposes.

Fourth, there are the district court judges, who are in a strategic position where they can order the school boards to act, or sabotage the Supreme Court order by employing all the delays that the technicalities of the law afford. Then there are the courts of appeals, which must review the decisions of the district judges, and which have generally taken a conscientious view of their obligation to enforce the Supreme Court's ruling.

Finally, there is the Supreme Court itself, which temporized for a time after 1954 and tried to stay above the battle, but which since 1958 has accepted the obligation to review lower court decisions and to implement its original 1954 decision—a task which may well take a generation to complete.

PROTECTION OF PROPERTY RIGHTS

By a variety of provisions the Constitution protects private property rights against government action. Both Federal and state governments have the power of eminent domain, that is, to take private property which is needed for a public purpose. But the Fifth Amendment requires Congress to give "just compensation" for property so taken, and the states have the same obligation under the due process clause.

The states are forbidden by Article I, section 10, to pass any law "impairing the obligation of contracts." In the first half of the nineteenth century, the contract clause was the principal guarantee against public regulation, particularly since Chief Justice Marshall interpreted the clause to cover charters granted to corporations. But the present-day significance of the contract clause is not great.

The most general protection for property rights is found in the due process clauses of the Fifth and Fourteenth Amendments. Beginning in the 1880s the Supreme Court developed a very strong laissez-faire bias in applying the due process test to state economic legislation. Among the important decisions striking down state regulation of private enterprise were *Lochner v. New York* (1905), in which a state 10-hour law for bakers was declared unconstitutional, and *Adkins v. Children's Hospital* (1923), voiding a District of Columbia minimum wage law for women. The Court was also during this period quite unfriendly to price control legislation. However, in 1934 the Court admitted that the states could regulate the price of milk, and in 1937 state minimum wage laws were approved. Since that time the Court has almost never struck down economic regulatory legislation, either Federal or state, on due process grounds.

SUMMARY

The maintenance of political and civil liberties is an indispensable condition to the successful operation of a democratic form of government. These liberties have a firm foundation in the American Constitution, but it requires more than words on parchment to give them reality. First of all, citizens must be able to defend their rights at the ballot box. The limitations on Negro voting in many states long supported racial discrimination in other fields. With the vote, any group is in a position to defend its own rights.

Second, defense of individual liberties requires action by the courts. They have to interpret the established constitutional principles and apply them to the constantly new problems of suppression or discrimination which arise. They have to be strong enough to defend the constitutional freedoms of unpopular persons.

Third, the principles of an open society must be generally accepted. It has taken many centuries to develop such concepts as due process of law, equal protection of the laws, freedom of speech and press, and the guarantee against taking of property without just compensation. In times of stress there are always temptations to abandon the rule of law and to revert to the methods of direct action or revenge or violence. The Constitution has provided a worthy guide for American democracy in both good and bad times.

Review Questions

1. How does the Constitution guarantee the right to vote?

2. Under what conditions are literacy tests a constitutional limitation on the franchise?

3. Do constitutional protections apply to voting in primary elections?

4. What is the purpose of the "clear and present danger" test?

5. Why has censorship been regarded as such a serious form of limitation on expression of opinion?

6. Why is it not an unconstitutional restriction on free speech and press to punish libel and slander?

7. What is the constitutional justification for actions taken by Congress against the Communist Party?

8. How have the protections of the First Amendment, which applies specifically to Congress, been made applicable to the states?

9. What limits has the Supreme Court appeared to set on public financial aid to church schools or religious programs in public schools?

10. What have been the problems in enforcement of the Supreme Court's decision declaring segregation in the public schools unconstitutional?

For Further Reading

BARTH, ALAN: *Government by Investigation*, The Viking Press, Inc., New York, 1955.

BEARD, CHARLES A.: *The Supreme Court and the Constitution*, Prentice-Hall, Inc., Englewood Cliffs, N.J., 1962.

BLACK, CHARLES L., JR.: *The People and the Court*, The Macmillan Company, New York, 1960.

BROWN, RALPH S., JR.: *Loyalty and Security*, Yale University Press, New Haven, Conn., 1958.

CARR, ROBERT K.: *The Supreme Court and Judicial Review*, Holt, Rinehart and Winston, Inc., New York, 1942.

CHAFEE, ZECHARIAH, JR.: *Free Speech in the United States*, Harvard University Press, Cambridge, Mass., 1941.

CORWIN, EDWARD S.: *The President: Office and Powers*, 4th ed., New York University Press, New York, 1957.

FELLMAN, DAVID: *The Defendant's Rights*, Holt, Rinehart and Winston, Inc., New York, 1958.

FRANK, JOHN P.: *Marble Palace*, Alfred A. Knopf, Inc., New York, 1958.

FREUND, PAUL A.: *On Understanding the Supreme Court*, Little, Brown and Company, Boston, 1949.

GALLOWAY, GEORGE B.: *The Legislative Process in Congress*, Thomas Y. Crowell Company, New York, 1953.

HAND, LEARNED: *The Bill of Rights*, Harvard University Press, Cambridge, Mass., 1958.

HARRIS, JOSEPH P.: *The Advice and Consent of the Senate*, University of California Press, Berkeley, Calif., 1953.

HARRIS, ROBERT J.: *The Quest for Equality*, Louisiana State University Press, Baton Rouge, La., 1960.

HORN, ROBERT A.: *Groups and the Constitution*, Stanford University Press, Stanford, Calif., 1956.

HUGHES, CHARLES EVANS: *The Supreme Court of the United States*, Columbia University Press, New York, 1928.

HYMAN, SIDNEY: *The American President*, Harper & Row, Publishers, Incorporated, New York, 1954.

KONVITZ, MILTON R.: *Fundamental Liberties of a Free People*, Cornell University Press, Ithaca, N.Y., 1957.

MCCLOSKY, ROBERT G.: *The American Supreme Court,* The University of Chicago Press, Chicago, 1960.

MEIKLEJOHN, ALEXANDER: *Political Freedom,* Harper & Row, Publishers, Incorporated, New York, 1960.

MENDELSON, WALLACE: *Justices Black and Frankfurter,* The University of Chicago Press, Chicago, 1961.

MURPHY, WALTER F.: *Congress and the Court,* The University of Chicago Press, Chicago, 1962.

NEUSTADT, RICHARD E.: *Presidential Power,* John Wiley & Sons, Inc., New York, 1960.

PELTASON, JACK: *58 Lonely Men,* Harcourt, Brace & World, Inc., New York, 1961.

PRITCHETT, C. HERMAN: *The American Constitution,* McGraw-Hill Book Company, Inc., New York, 1959.

————: *The Roosevelt Court,* The Macmillan Company, New York, 1948.

ROSSITER, CLINTON: *The American Presidency,* Harcourt, Brace & World, Inc., New York, 1956.

TAYLOR, TELFORD: *Grand Inquest: The Story of Congressional Investigations,* Simon and Schuster, Inc., New York, 1955.

WARREN, CHARLES: *The Supreme Court in United States History,* 2 vols., Little, Brown and Company, Boston, 1947.

WILMERDING, LUCIUS, JR.: *The Electoral College,* Rutgers University Press, New Brunswick, N.J., 1958.

Appendix

We the people of the United States, in Order to form a more perfect Union, establish Justice, insure domestic Tranquility, provide for the common defence, promote the general Welfare, and secure the Blessings of Liberty to ourselves and our Posterity, do ordain and establish this CONSTITUTION for the United States of America.

ARTICLE I

Section 1. All legislative Powers herein granted shall be vested in a Congress of the United States, which shall consist of a Senate and House of Representatives.

Section 2. (1) The House of Representatives shall be composed of Members chosen every second Year by the People of the several States, and the Electors in each State shall have the Qualifications requisite for Electors of the most numerous Branch of the State Legislature.

(2) No Person shall be a Representative who shall not have attained to the Age of twenty five Years, and been seven Years a Citizen of the United States, and who shall not, when elected, be an Inhabitant of that State in which he shall be chosen.

(3) Representatives and direct Taxes[1] shall be apportioned among the several States which may be included within this Union, accord-

---

[1] Modified as to direct taxes by the Sixteenth Amendment.

ing to their respective Numbers, which shall be determined by adding to the whole Number of free Persons, including those bound to Service for a Term of Years, and excluding Indians not taxed, three fifths of all other Persons.[2] The actual Enumeration shall be made within three Years after the first Meeting of the Congress of the United States, and within every subsequent Term of ten Years, in such Manner as they shall by Law direct. The Number of Representatives shall not exceed one for every thirty Thousand, but each State shall have at Least one Representative; and until such enumeration shall be made, the State of New Hampshire shall be entitled to chuse three, Massachusetts eight, Rhode-Island and Providence Plantations one, Connecticut five, New-York six, New Jersey four, Pennsylvania eight, Delaware one, Maryland six, Virginia ten, North Carolina five, South Carolina five, and Georgia three.

(4) When vacancies happen in the Representation from any State, the Executive Authority thereof shall issue Writs of Election to fill such Vacancies.

(5) The House of Representatives shall chuse their Speaker and other Officers; and shall have the sole Power of Impeachment.

Section 3. (1) The Senate of the United States shall be composed of two Senators from each State, chosen by the Legislature thereof,[3] for six Years; and each Senator shall have one Vote.

(2) Immediately after they shall be assembled in Consequence of the first Election, they shall be divided as equally as may be into three Classes. The Seats of the Senators of the first Class shall be vacated at the Expiration of the second Year, of the second Class at the Expiration of the fourth Year, and of the third Class at the Expiration of the sixth Year, so that one third may be chosen every second Year; and if Vacancies happen by Resignation, or otherwise, during the Recess of the Legislature of any State, the Executive thereof may make temporary Appointments until the next Meeting of the Legislature, which shall then fill such Vacancies.

(3) No Person shall be a Senator who shall not have attained to the Age of thirty Years, and been nine Years a Citizen of the United States, and who shall not, when elected, be an Inhabitant of that State for which he shall be chosen.

(4) The Vice President of the United States shall be President of the Senate, but shall have no Vote, unless they be equally divided.

[2] Replaced by the Fourteenth Amendment.
[3] Modified by the Seventeenth Amendment.

(5) The Senate shall chuse their other Officers, and also a President pro tempore, in the Absence of the Vice President, or when he shall exercise the Office of President of the United States.

(6) The Senate shall have the sole Power to try all Impeachments. When sitting for that Purpose, they shall be on Oath or Affirmation. When the President of the United States is tried, the Chief Justice shall preside: And no Person shall be convicted without the Concurrence of two thirds of the Members present.

(7) Judgment in Cases of Impeachment shall not extend further than to removal from Office, and disqualification to hold and enjoy any Office of honor, Trust or Profit under the United States: but the Party convicted shall nevertheless be liable and subject to Indictment, Trial, Judgment and Punishment, according to Law.

Section 4. (1) The Times, Places and Manner of holding Elections for Senators and Representatives, shall be prescribed in each State by the Legislature thereof; but the Congress may at any time by Law make or alter such Regulations, except as to the Places of chusing Senators.

(2) The Congress shall assemble at least once in every Year, and such Meeting shall be on the first Monday in December, unless they shall by Law appoint a different Day.[4]

Section 5. (1) Each House shall be the Judge of the Elections, Returns and Qualifications of its own Members, and a Majority of each shall constitute a Quorum to do Business; but a smaller Number may adjourn from day to day, and may be authorized to compel the attendance of absent Members, in such Manner, and under such Penalties as each House may provide.

(2) Each House may determine the Rules of its Proceedings, punish its Members for Disorderly Behaviour, and, with the Concurrence of two thirds, expel a Member.

(3) Each House shall keep a Journal of its Proceedings, and from time to time publish the same, excepting such Parts as may in their Judgment require Secrecy; and the Yeas and Nays of the Members of either House on any question shall, at the Desire of one fifth of those Present, be entered on the Journal.

(4) Neither House, during the Session of Congress, shall, without the Consent of the other, adjourn for more than three days, nor to any other Place than that in which the two Houses shall be sitting.

Section 6. (1) The Senators and Representatives shall receive a

[4] Modified by the Twentieth Amendment.

Compensation for their Services, to be ascertained by Law, and paid out of the Treasury of the United States. They shall in all Cases, except Treason, Felony and Breach of the Peace, be privileged from Arrest during their Attendance at the Session of their respective Houses, and in going to and returning from the same; and for any Speech or Debate in either House, they shall not be questioned in any other Place.

(2) No Senator or Representative shall, during the Time for which he was elected, be appointed to any civil Office under the Authority of the United States, which shall have been created, or the Emoluments whereof shall have been encreased during such time; and no Person holding any Office under the United States, shall be a member of either House during his Continuance in Office.

Section 7. (1) All Bills for raising Revenue shall originate in the House of Representatives; but the Senate may propose or concur with Amendments as on other Bills.

(2) Every Bill which shall have passed the House of Representatives and the Senate, shall, before it become a Law, be presented to the President of the United States; If he approve he shall sign it, but if not he shall return it, with his Objections to that House in which it shall have originated, who shall enter the Objections at large on their Journal, and proceed to reconsider it. If after such Reconsideration two thirds of that House shall agree to pass the Bill, it shall be sent, together with the Objections, to the other House, by which it shall likewise be reconsidered, and if approved by two thirds of that House, it shall become a Law. But in all such Cases the Votes of both Houses shall be determined by yeas and Nays, and the Names of the Persons voting for and against the Bill shall be entered on the Journal of each House respectively. If any Bill shall not be returned by the President within ten Days (Sundays excepted) after it shall have been presented to him, the same shall be a Law, in like Manner as if he had signed it, unless the Congress by their Adjournment prevent its Return, in which Case it shall not be a Law.

(3) Every Order, Resolution, or Vote to which the Concurrence of the Senate and House of Representatives may be necessary (except on a question of Adjournment) shall be presented to the President of the United States; and before the same shall take Effect, shall be approved by him, or being disapproved by him, shall be repassed by two thirds of the Senate and House of Representatives, according to the Rules and Limitations prescribed in the Case of a Bill.

Section 8. The Congress shall have Power (1) To lay and col¹

Taxes, Duties, Imposts and Excises, to pay the Debts and provide for the common Defence and general Welfare of the United States; but all Duties, Imposts and Excises shall be uniform throughout the United States;

(2) To borrow Money on the credit of the United States;

(3) To regulate Commerce with foreign Nations, and among the several States, and with the Indian Tribes;

(4) To establish an uniform Rule of Naturalization, and uniform Laws on the subject of Bankruptcies throughout the United States;

(5) To coin Money, regulate the Value thereof, and of foreign Coin, and fix the Standard of Weights and Measures;

(6) To provide for the Punishment of counterfeiting the Securities and current Coin of the United States;

(7) To establish Post Offices and post Roads;

(8) To promote the Progress of Science and useful Arts, by securing for limited Times to Authors and Inventors the exclusive Right to their respective Writings and Discoveries;

(9) To constitute Tribunals inferior to the supreme Court;

(10) To define and punish Piracies and Felonies committed on the high Seas, and Offences against the Law of Nations;

(11) To declare War, grant Letters of Marque and Reprisal, and make Rules concerning Captures on Land and Water;

(12) To raise and support Armies, but no Appropriation of Money to that Use shall be for a longer Term than two Years;

(13) To provide and maintain a Navy;

(14) To make Rules for the Government and Regulation of the land and naval Forces;

(15) To provide for calling forth the Militia to execute the Laws of the Union, suppress Insurrections and repel Invasions;

(16) To provide for organizing, arming, and disciplining, the Militia, and for governing such Part of them as may be employed in the Service of the United States, reserving to the States respectively, the Appointment of the Officers, and the Authority of training the Militia according to the discipline prescribed by Congress;

(17) To exercise exclusive Legislation in all Cases whatsoever, over such District (not exceeding ten Miles square) as may, by Cession of particular States, and the Acceptance of Congress, become the Seat of the Government of the United States, and to exercise like Authority over all Places purchased by the Consent of the Legislature of the State in which the same shall be, for the Erection of Forts, Magazines, Arsenals, dock-Yards, and other needful Buildings;—And

(18) To make all Laws which shall be necessary and proper for carrying into Execution the foregoing Powers, and all other Powers vested by this Constitution in the Government of the United States, or in any Department or Officer thereof.

Section 9. (1) The Migration or Importation of such Persons as any of the States now existing shall think proper to admit, shall not be prohibited by the Congress prior to the Year one thousand eight hundred and eight, but a Tax or duty may be imposed on such Importation, not exceeding ten dollars for each Person.

(2) The Privilege of the Writ of Habeas Corpus shall not be suspended, unless when in Cases of Rebellion or Invasion the public Safety may require it.

(3) No Bill of Attainder or ex post facto Law shall be passed.

(4) No Capitation, or other direct, Tax shall be laid, unless in Proportion to the Census or Enumeration herein before directed to be taken.[5]

(5) No Tax or Duty shall be laid on Articles exported from any State.

(6) No Preference shall be given by any Regulation of Commerce or Revenue to the Ports of one State over those of another: nor shall Vessels bound to, or from, one State, be obliged to enter, clear, or pay Duties in another.

(7) No Money shall be drawn from the Treasury, but in Consequence of Appropriations made by Law; and a regular Statement and Account of the Receipts and Expenditures of all public Money shall be published from time to time.

(8) No Title of Nobility shall be granted by the United States: And no Person holding any Office of Profit or Trust under them, shall, without the Consent of the Congress, accept of any present, Emolument, Office, or Title, of any kind whatever, from any King, Prince, or foreign State.

Section 10. (1) No State shall enter into any Treaty, Alliance, or Confederation; grant Letters of Marque and Reprisal; coin Money; emit Bills of Credit; make any Thing but gold and silver Coin a Tender in Payment of Debts; pass any Bill of Attainder, ex post facto Law, or Law impairing the Obligation of Contracts, or grant any Title of Nobility.

(2) No State shall, without the Consent of the Congress, lay any Imposts or Duties on Imports or Exports, except what may be absolutely necessary for executing its inspection Laws; and the net Produce of all

[5] Modified by the Sixteenth Amendment.

Duties and Imposts, laid by any State on Imports or Exports, shall be for the Use of the Treasury of the United States; and all such Laws shall be subject to the Revision and Controul of the Congress.

(3) No State shall, without the Consent of Congress, lay any Duty of Tonnage, keep Troops, or Ships of War in time of Peace, enter into any Agreement or Compact with another State, or with a foreign Power, or engage in War, unless actually invaded, or in such imminent Danger as will not admit of delay.

ARTICLE II

Section 1. (1) The executive Power shall be vested in a President of the United States of America. He shall hold his Office during the Term of four Years, and, together with the Vice President, chosen for the same Term, be elected, as follows.

(2) Each State shall appoint, in such Manner as the Legislature thereof may direct, a Number of Electors, equal to the whole Number of Senators and Representatives to which the State may be entitled in the Congress: but no Senator or Representative, or Person holding an Office of Trust or Profit under the United States, shall be appointed an Elector.

(3) The Electors shall meet in their respective States, and vote by Ballot for two Persons, of whom one at least shall not be an Inhabitant of the same State with themselves. And they shall make a List of all the Persons voted for, and of the Number of Votes for each; which List they shall sign and certify, and transmit sealed to the Seat of Government of the United States, directed to the President of the Senate. The President of the Senate shall, in the Presence of the Senate and House of Representatives, open all the Certificates, and the Votes shall then be counted. The Person having the greatest Number of Votes shall be the President, if such Number be a Majority of the whole Number of Electors appointed; and if there be more than one who have such Majority, and have an equal Number of Votes, then the House of Representatives shall immediately chuse by Ballot one of them for President; and if no Person have a Majority, then from the five highest on the List the said House shall in like Manner chuse the President. But in chusing the President, the Votes shall be taken by States, the Representation from each State having one Vote; A quorum for this Purpose shall consist of a Member or Members from two thirds of the States, and a Majority of all the States shall be necessary to a Choice.

In every Case, after the Choice of the President, the Person having the greatest Number of Votes of the Electors shall be the Vice President. But if there should remain two or more who have equal Votes, the Senate shall chuse from them by Ballot the Vice President.[6]

(4) The Congress may determine the Time of chusing the Electors, and the Day on which they shall give their Votes; which Day shall be the same throughout the United States.

(5) No Person except a natural born Citizen, or a Citizen of the United States, at the time of the Adoption of this Constitution, shall be eligible to the Office of President; neither shall any Person be eligible to that Office who shall not have attained to the Age of thirty five Years, and been fourteen Years a Resident within the United States.

(6) In Case of the Removal of the President from Office, or of his Death, Resignation, or Inability to discharge the Powers and Duties of the said Office, the Same shall devolve on the Vice President, and the Congress may by Law provide for the Case of Removal, Death, Resignation, or Inability, both of the President and Vice President, declaring what Officer shall then act as President, and such Officer shall act accordingly, until the Disability be removed, or a President shall be elected.

(7) The President shall, at stated Times, receive for his Services, a Compensation, which shall neither be encreased nor diminished during the Period for which he shall have been elected, and he shall not receive within that Period any other Emolument from the United States, or any of them.

(8) Before he enter on the Execution of his Office, he shall take the following Oath or Affirmation:—"I do solemnly swear (or affirm) that I will faithfully execute the Office of President of the United States, and will to the best of my Ability, preserve, protect and defend the Constitution of the United States."

Section 2. (1) The President shall be Commander in Chief of the Army and Navy of the United States, and of the Militia of the several States, when called into the actual Service of the United States; he may require the Opinion, in writing, of the principal Officer in each of the executive Departments, upon any Subject relating to the Duties of their respective Offices, and he shall have Power to grant Reprieves and Pardons for Offences against the United States, except in Cases of Impeachment.

(2) He shall have Power, by and with the Advice and Consent of

[6] This paragraph was replaced in 1804 by the Twelfth Amendment.

the Senate, to make Treaties, provided two thirds of the Senators present concur; and he shall nominate, and by and with the Advice and Consent of the Senate, shall appoint Ambassadors, other public Ministers and Consuls, Judges of the supreme Court, and all other Officers of the United States, whose Appointments are not herein otherwise provided for, and which shall be established by Law: but the Congress may by Law vest the Appointment of such inferior Officers, as they think proper, in the President alone, in the Courts of Law, or in the Heads of Departments.

(3) The President shall have Power to fill up all Vacancies that may happen during the Recess of the Senate, by granting Commissions which shall expire at the End of their next Session.

Section 3. He shall from time to time give to the Congress Information of the State of the Union, and recommend to their Consideration such Measures as he shall judge necessary and expedient; he may, on extraordinary Occasions, convene both Houses, or either of them, and in Case of Disagreement between them, with Respect to the Time of Adjournment, he may adjourn them to such Time as he shall think proper; he shall receive Ambassadors and other public Ministers; he shall take Care that the Laws be faithfully executed, and shall Commission all the Officers of the United States.

Section 4. The President, Vice President and all civil Officers of the United States, shall be removed from Office on Impeachment for, and Conviction of, Treason, Bribery, or other high Crimes and Misdemeanors.

ARTICLE III

Section 1. The Judicial Power of the United States, shall be vested in one supreme Court, and in such inferior Courts as the Congress may from time to time ordain and establish. The Judges, both of the supreme and inferior Courts, shall hold their Offices during good Behaviour, and shall, at stated Times, receive for their Services, a Compensation, which shall not be diminished during their Continuance in Office.

Section 2. (1) The judicial Power shall extend to all Cases, in Law and Equity, arising under this Constitution, the Laws of the United States, and Treaties made, or which shall be made, under their Authority;—to all Cases affecting Ambassadors, other public Ministers and Consuls;—to all Cases of admiralty and maritime Jurisdiction;—to Controversies to which the United States shall be a Party;—to Controversies between two or more States;—between a State and Citizens of another State;[7]—between Citizens of different States;—between Citizens of the same State claiming Lands under Grants of different States, and between a State, or the Citizens thereof, and foreign States, Citizens or Subjects.

(2) In all Cases affecting Ambassadors, other public Ministers and Consuls, and those in which a State shall be Party, the supreme Court shall have original Jurisdiction. In all the other Cases before mentioned, the Supreme Court shall have appellate Jurisdiction, both as to Law and Fact, with such Exceptions, and under such Regulations as the Congress shall make.

(3) The Trial of all Crimes, except in Cases of impeachment, shall be by Jury; and such Trial shall be held in the State where the said Crimes shall have been committed; but when not committed within any State, the Trial shall be at such Place or Places as the Congress may by Law have directed.

Section 3. (1) Treason against the United States, shall consist only in levying War against them, or in adhering to their Enemies, giving them Aid and Comfort. No Person shall be convicted of Treason unless on the Testimony of two Witnesses to the same overt Act, or on Confession in open Court.

(2) The Congress shall have Power to declare the Punishment of Treason, but no Attainder of Treason shall work Corruption of Blood, or Forfeiture except during the Life of the Person attainted.

ARTICLE IV

Section 1. Full Faith and Credit shall be given in each State to the public Acts, Records, and judicial Proceedings of every other State. And the Congress may by general Laws prescribe the Manner in which such Acts, Records and Proceedings shall be proved, and the Effect thereof.

Section 2. (1) The Citizens of each State shall be entitled to all Privileges and Immunities of Citizens in the several States.

(2) A Person charged in any State with Treason, Felony, or other Crime, who shall flee from Justice, and be found in another State, shall

[7] Restricted by the Eleventh Amendment.

on Demand of the executive Authority of the State from which he fled, be delivered up, to be removed to the State having Jurisdiction of the Crime.

(3) No Person held to Service or Labour in one State, under the Laws thereof, escaping into another, shall, in Consequence of any Law or Regulation therein, be discharged from such Service or Labour, but shall be delivered up on Claim of the Party to whom such Service or Labour may be due.

Section 3. (1) New States may be admitted by the Congress into this Union; but no new State shall be formed or erected within the Jurisdiction of any other States; nor any State be formed by the Junction of two or more States, or Parts of States, without the Consent of the Legislatures of the States concerned as well as of the Congress.

(2) The Congress shall have Power to dispose of and make all needful Rules and Regulations respecting the Territory or other Property belonging to the United States; and nothing in this Constitution shall be so construed as to Prejudice any Claims of the United States, or of any particular State.

Section 4. The United States shall guarantee to every State in this Union a Republican Form of Government, and shall protect each of them against Invasion; and on Application of the Legislature, or of the Executive (when the Legislature cannot be convened) against domestic Violence.

ARTICLE V

The Congress, whenever two thirds of both Houses shall deem it necessary, shall propose Amendments to this Constitution, or, on the Application of the Legislatures of two thirds of the several States, shall call a Convention for proposing Amendments, which, in either Case, shall be valid to all Intents and Purposes, as Part of this Constitution, when ratified by the Legislatures of three fourths of the several States, or by Conventions in three fourths thereof, as the one or the other Mode of Ratification may be proposed by the Congress; Provided that no Amendment which may be made prior to the Year One thousand eight hundred and eight shall in any Manner affect the first and fourth Clauses in the Ninth Section of the first Article; and that no State, without its Consent, shall be deprived of its equal Suffrage in the Senate.

ARTICLE VI

(1) All Debts contracted and Engagements entered into, before the Adoption of this Constitution, shall be as valid against the United States under this Constitution, as under the Confederation.

(2) This Constitution, and the Laws of the United States which shall be made in Pursuance thereof; and all Treaties made, or which shall be made, under the Authority of the United States, shall be the supreme Law of the Land; and the Judges in every State shall be bound thereby, any Thing in the Constitution or Laws of any State to the Contrary notwithstanding.

(3) The Senators and Representatives before mentioned, and the Members of the several State Legislatures, and all executive and judicial Officers, both of the United States and of the several States, shall be bound by Oath or Affirmation, to support this Constitution; but no religious Test shall ever be required as a Qualification to any Office or Public Trust under the United States.

ARTICLE VII

The Ratification of the Conventions of nine States, shall be sufficient for the Establishment of this Constitution between the States so ratifying the Same.

AMENDMENTS

AMENDMENT I

Congress shall make no law respecting an establishment of religion, or prohibiting the free exercise thereof; or abridging the freedom of speech, or of the press; or the right of the people peaceably to assemble, and to petition the Government for a redress of grievances.

AMENDMENT II

A well regulated Militia, being necessary to the security of a free State, the right of the people to keep and bear Arms, shall not be infringed.

AMENDMENT III

No Soldier shall, in time of peace be quartered in any house, without the consent of the Owner, nor in time of war, but in a manner to be prescribed by law.

AMENDMENT IV

The right of the people to be secure in their persons, houses, papers, and effects, against unreasonable searches and seizures, shall not be violated, and no Warrants shall issue, but upon probable cause, supported by Oath or affirmation, and particularly describing the place to be searched, and the persons or things to be seized.

AMENDMENT V

No person shall be held to answer for a capital, or otherwise infamous crime, unless on a presentment or indictment of a Grand Jury, except in cases arising in the land or naval forces, or in the Militia, when in actual service in time of War or public danger; nor shall any person be subject for the same offence to be twice put in jeopardy of life or limb; nor shall be compelled in any criminal case to be a witness against himself; nor be deprived of life, liberty, or property, without due process of law; nor shall private property be taken for public use, without just compensation.

AMENDMENT VI

In all criminal prosecutions the accused shall enjoy the right to a speedy and public trial, by an impartial jury of the State and district wherein the crime shall have been committed, which district shall have been previously ascertained by law, and to be informed of the nature and cause of the accusation; to be confronted with the witnesses against him; to have compulsory process for obtaining witnesses in his favor, and to have the Assistance of Counsel for his defence.

AMENDMENT VII

In suits at common law, where the value in controversy shall exceed twenty dollars, the right of trial by jury shall be preserved, and no fact tried by a jury shall be otherwise re-examined in any Court of the United States, than according to the rules of the common law.

AMENDMENT VIII

Excessive bail shall not be required, nor excessive fines imposed, nor cruel and unusual punishments inflicted.

AMENDMENT IX

The enumeration in the Constitution, of certain rights, shall not be construed to deny or disparage others retained by the people.

AMENDMENT X

The powers not delegated to the United States by the Constitution, not prohibited by it to the States, are reserved to the States respectively, or to the people.

[The first ten Amendments were adopted in 1791.]

AMENDMENT XI

The Judicial power of the United States shall not be construed to extend to any suit in law or equity, commenced or prosecuted against one of the United States by Citizens of another State, or by Citizens or Subjects of any Foreign State. [Adopted in 1798.]

AMENDMENT XII

The Electors shall meet in their respective states, and vote by ballot for President and Vice-President, one of whom, at least, shall not be an inhabitant of the same state with themselves; they shall name in their ballots the person voted for as President, and in distinct ballots the person voted for as Vice-President, and they shall make distinct lists of all persons voted for as President, and of all persons voted for as Vice-President, and of the number of votes for each, which lists they shall sign and certify, and transmit sealed to the seat of the government of the United States, directed to the President of the Senate; —The President of the Senate shall, in the presence of the Senate and House of Representatives, open all the certificates and the votes shall then be counted;—The person having the greatest number of votes for President, shall be the President, if such number be a majority of the whole number of Electors appointed; and if no person have such majority, then from the persons having the highest numbers not exceeding three on the list of those voted for as President, the House of Representatives shall choose immediately, by ballot, the President. But in choosing the President, the votes shall be taken by states, the representation from each state having one vote; a quorum for this purpose shall consist of a member or members from two-thirds of the states, and a majority of all the states shall be necessary to a choice. And if the House of Representatives shall not choose a President whenever the right of choice shall devolve upon them, before the fourth day of March next following, then the Vice-President shall act as President, as in the case of the death or other constitutional disability of the President.—The person having the greatest number of votes as Vice-President, shall be the Vice-President, if such number be a majority of the whole number of Electors appointed, and if no person have a majority, then from the two highest numbers on the list, the Senate shall choose the Vice-President; a quorum for the purpose shall consist of two-thirds of the whole number of Senators, and a majority of the whole number shall be necessary to a choice. But no person constitutionally ineligible to the office of President shall be eligible to that of Vice-President of the United States. [Adopted in 1804.]

AMENDMENT XIII

Section 1. Neither slavery nor involuntary servitude, except as a punishment for crime whereof the party shall have been duly convicted, shall exist within the United States, or any place subject to their jurisdiction.

Section 2. Congress shall have power to enforce this article by appropriate legislation. [Adopted in 1865.]

AMENDMENT XIV

Section 1. All persons born or naturalized in the United States, and subject to the jurisdiction thereof, are citizens of the United States and of the State wherein they reside. No State shall make or enforce any law which shall abridge the privileges or immunities of citizens of the United States; nor shall any State deprive any person of life, liberty, or property, without due process of law; nor deny to any person within its jurisdiction the equal protection of the laws.

Section 2. Representatives shall be apportioned among the several States according to their respective numbers, counting the whole number of persons in each State, excluding Indians not taxed. But when the right to vote at any election for the choice of electors for President and Vice President of the United States, Representatives in Congress, the Executive and Judicial officers of a State, or the members of the Legislature thereof, is denied to any of the male inhabitants of such State, being twenty-one years of age, and citizens of the United States, or in any way abridged, except for participation in rebellion, or other crime, the basis of representation therein shall be reduced in the proportion which the number of such male citizens shall bear to the whole number of male citizens twenty-one years of age in such State.

Section 3. No person shall be a Senator or Representative in Congress, or elector of President and Vice President, or hold any office, civil or military, under the United States, or under any State, who, having previously taken an oath, as a member of Congress, or as an officer of the United States, or as a member of any State legislature, or as an executive or judicial officer of any State, to support the Constitution of the United States, shall have engaged in insurrection or rebellion against the same, or given aid or comfort to the enemies thereof. But Congress may by a vote of two-thirds of each House, remove such disability.

Section 4. The validity of the public debt of the United States, authorized by law, including debts incurred for payment of pensions and bounties for services in suppressing insurrection or rebellion, shall not be questioned. But neither the United States nor any State shall assume or pay any debt or obligation incurred in aid of insurrection or rebellion against the United States, or any claim for the loss or emancipation of any slave; but all such debts, obligations and claims shall be held illegal and void.

Section 5. The Congress shall have power to enforce, by appropriate legislation, the provisions of this article. [Adopted in 1868.]

AMENDMENT XV

Section 1. The right of citizens of the United States to vote shall not be denied or abridged by the United States or by any State on account of race, color, or previous condition of servitude.

Section 2. The Congress shall have power to enforce this article by appropriate legislation. [Adopted in 1870.]

AMENDMENT XVI

The Congress shall have power to lay and collect taxes on incomes, from whatever source derived, without apportionment among the several States, and without regard to any census or enumeration. [Adopted in 1913.]

AMENDMENT XVII

The Senate of the United States shall be composed of two Senators from each State, elected by the people thereof, for six years; and each Senator shall have one vote. The electors in each State shall have the qualifications requisite for electors of the most numerous branch of the State legislatures.

When vacancies happen in the representation of any State in the Senate, the executive authority of such State shall issue writs of election to fill such vacancies: *Provided,* That the legislature of any State may empower the executive thereof to make temporary appointments until the people fill the vacancies by election as the legislature may direct.

This amendment shall not be so construed as to affect the election or term of any Senator chosen before it becomes valid as part of the Constitution. [Adopted in 1913.]

AMENDMENT XVIII

Section 1. After one year from the ratification of this article the manufacture, sale, or transportation of intoxicating liquors within, the importation thereof into, or the exportation thereof from the United States and all territory subject to the jurisdiction thereof for beverage purposes is hereby prohibited.

Section 2. The Congress and the several States shall have concurrent power to enforce this article by appropriate legislation.

Section 3. This article shall be inoperative unless it shall have been ratified as an amendment to the Constitution by the legislatures of the several States, as provided in the Constitution, within seven years from the date of the submission hereof to the States by the Congress. [Adopted in 1919.]

AMENDMENT XIX

The right of citizens of the United States to vote shall not be denied or abridged by the United States or by any State on account of sex. Congress shall have power to enforce this article by appropriate legislation. [Adopted in 1920.]

AMENDMENT XX

Section 1. The terms of the President and Vice President shall end at noon on the 20th day of January, and the terms of Senators and Representatives at noon on the 3d day of January, of the years in which such terms would have ended if this article had not been ratified; and the terms of their successors shall then begin.

Section 2. The Congress shall assemble at least once in every year, and such meeting shall begin at noon on the 3d day of January, unless they shall by law appoint a different day.

Section 3. If, at the time fixed for the beginning of the term of the President, the President elect shall have died, the Vice President elect shall become President. If a President shall not have been chosen before the time fixed for the beginning of his term, or if the President elect shall have failed to qualify, then the Vice President elect shall act as President until a President shall have qualified; and the Congress may by law provided for the case wherein neither a President elect nor a Vice President elect shall have qualified, declaring who shall then act as President, or the manner in which one who is to act shall be selected, and such person shall act accordingly until a President or Vice President shall have qualified.

Section 4. The Congress may by law provide for the case of the death of any of the persons from whom the House of Representatives may choose a President whenever the right of choice shall have devolved upon them, and for the case of the death of any of the persons from whom the Senate may choose a Vice President whenever the right of choice shall have devolved upon them.

Section 5. Sections 1 and 2 shall take effect on the 15th day of October following the ratification of this article.

Section 6. This article shall be inoperative unless it shall have been ratified as an amendment to the Constitution by the legislatures of three-fourths of the several States within seven years from the date of its submission. [Adopted in 1933.]

AMENDMENT XXI

Section 1. The eighteenth article of amendment to the Constitution of the United States is hereby repealed.

Section 2. The transportation or importation into any State, Territory, or possession of the United States for delivery or use therein of intoxicating liquors, in violation of the laws thereof, is hereby prohibited.

Section 3. This article shall be inoperative unless it shall have been ratified as an amendment to the Constitution by conventions in the several States, as provided in the Constitution, within seven years from the date of the submission hereof to the States by the Congress. [Adopted in 1933.]

AMENDMENT XXII

Section 1. No person shall be elected to the office of the President more than twice, and no person who has held the office of President, or acted as President, for more than two years of a term to which some other person was elected President shall be elected to the office of the President more than once. But this Article shall not apply to any persons holding the office of President when this Article was proposed by the Congress, and shall not prevent any person who may be holding the office of President, or acting as President, during the term within which this Article becomes operative from holding the office of President or acting as President during the remainder of such term.

Section 2. This Article shall be inoperative unless it shall have been ratified as an amendment to the Constitution by the legislatures of three-fourths of the several States within seven years from the date of its submission to the states by the Congress. [Adopted in 1951.]

AMENDMENT XXIII

Section 1. The District constituting the seat of Government of the United States shall appoint in such manner as the Congress may direct:

A number of electors of President and Vice President equal to the whole number of Senators and Representatives in Congress to which the District would be entitled if it were a State, but in no event more than the least populous State; they shall be in addition to those appointed by the States, but they shall be considered, for the purposes of the election of President and Vice President, to be electors appointed by a State; and they shall meet in the District and perform such duties as provided by the twelfth article of amendment.

Section 2. The Congress shall have power to enforce this article by appropriate legislation. [Adopted in 1961.]

Index